Sophie Robehmed
Illustrated by **Karim Al-Dahdah**

Only in Dubai

AN ESSENTIAL GUIDE TO THE EMIRATE'S EXPATS

turning**point**
BOOKS

Published by Turning Point Books
14th Floor, Concorde Building, Dunan Street,
Verdun, Beirut, Lebanon
PO Box 11-4932
Tel: 00961 1 752 100
www.tpbooksonline.com

First edition: February 2015

Text copyright © Sophie Robehmed, 2015
Illustrations copyright © Karim Al-Dahdah, 2015
Layout and graphic design copyright © Turning Point, 2015

Design and layout: Chantal Coroller
Editing: Jasmina Najjar
Printing: RAIDY | www.raidy.com

All rights reserved.

No part of this publication may be reproduced or submitted in any form or any means without the written permission of the publisher.

The characters illustrated in this book are solely fictitious and any resemblance or similarities to an existing personality is purely coincidental.

ISBN 978-9953-0-3061-6

About the Author

Sophie Robehmed is a British-Lebanese writer, journalist and nostalgic former Dubai expat. She has worked for the BBC, CNN, Channel 4 News, *The Guardian*, *The Independent*, *The Sunday Times*, *National Geographic Traveller*, *Reader's Digest*, *Gulf News*, *The National* and *Grazia Middle East* among others. She was shortlisted for 'Young Travel Writer of the Year' at the 2013 British Travel Press Awards. You can find her on Twitter @sophierobehmed.

About the Illustrator

Karim Al-Dahdah was born in Beirut, Lebanon, and started freelancing when he was still an undergraduate at the Académie Libanaise des Beaux-Arts. He received a master's degree in Illustration at the Savannah College of Art and Design and worked as an art director at a leading publisher in Chicago before opening his own illustration studio in Beirut. He illustrated several children's books as well as editorial, advertising and educational projects.

In 2013, he published his first authored children's story, the critically acclaimed, bilingual *Sitt Sobhiye and the Quest for the White Horse*. He currently resides in Montreal, Canada, where he actively pursues his freelance illustration career. His work can be seen on karimaldahdah.com.

For Mum, Dad, Chantal and Puppy, with all my love.

In loving memory of Granny and Liz.

"Life might be difficult for a year or two, but I would tough it out because living in a foreign country is one of those things that everyone should try at least once. My understanding was that it completed a person, sanding down the rough provincial edges and transforming you into a citizen of the world... What I found appealing in life abroad was the inevitable sense of helplessness it would inspire. Equally exciting would be the work involved in overcoming that helplessness. There would be a goal involved, and I like having goals."

David Sedaris, *Me Talk Pretty One Day*

Acknowledgements

I'd like to say a huge thank you to the Turning Point team, in particular Charlotte, Eleena, Sarah and Jasmina, for their enthusiasm, faith, and support in this project. Karim, for his incredibly imaginative illustrations, and Chantal, for her handsome design skills, both of which have really brought Dubai's expats to life. Annabel, for her wonderfully witty words. Dubai, and everyone I met along the way, for the memories, life lessons, laughs, and writing fodder. And last, but by no means least, thank you and the biggest love to my lovely mum, Caroline, dad, Georges, sister, Chantal, grandad, Puppy, and friend, Rich, for their endless love and for being so excited about the book. For always encouraging me, being there, and cracking me up. I am always grateful.

Foreword

In the 16 years that I've lived in the emirate, I've noticed that expats like to poke fun at themselves – and none more so than the Dubai expat. Perhaps we've had to grow a thick skin given that Dubai is the place that everyone loves, hates or, more usually, loves to hate.

Even if they've never been to Dubai, most people have a mental image of what the stereotypical 'Dubai expat' might be like and I'd bet my last dirham that, for most people, he'd be rich, brash and larger than life. He'd be an egotistical chap, who stuffs his beer belly into a Porsche 911 (that he's bought on credit) and brays into a couple of smartphones, while propping up the bar at his local golf club.

Or perhaps it would be the infamous Jumeirah Jane – a throwback from the 1980s: the artificially blonde airhead who lives in a sprawling villa in the residential district of Jumeirah, drives an expensive four-wheeler, is rude to the 'servants' and cares more about her tennis lessons, coffee mornings, facials and nail appointments than she does about her expat brat children.

Maybe those stereotypes were true once upon a time, but with Dubai's population growing faster than a new expat's waistline, you'll find far richer pickings these days. While we've always had the Culture Vultures, the Dubaiophiles, the Reluctant Expats, the Explorers and the Transients that Sophie mentions, we're seeing new categories of expats shaped by the ways in which the city has developed in the last decade.

First, and perhaps the most vocal, are the Foodies. Initially brought to the city by the explosion of celebrity restaurants, the Foodies are now becoming ever more competitive as the focus moves away from five-star restaurants to a more authentic 'farm to table' experience. Then there are the Yogis. These bendy beings are multiplying as more families settle here, and stay-at-home mums look for flexible jobs that they can fit around the children. We're also seeing the rise of the Start-Up Stars, who are taking advantage of easier and faster ways to set up and own a business in the city's free zones.

Meanwhile, our bombastic expat at the golf club has, these days, morphed into a younger version whose haunt is the city's many Friday brunches… but the less said about him, the better.

Annabel Kantaria, author and journalist, writes the Dubai Expat blog for *The Daily Telegraph*.

Preface

*O*nce upon a time, I have to admit that, just like the Reluctant Expat in this very book, I was supposed to be moving to Paris, but ended up in Dubai. Following a 'staffing error' in the City of Light, I applied, was offered, and accepted a magazine job in the emirate. The day after I signed the contract, Paris emailed to tell me that they finally had work for me. Instead of pursuing the 'je ne sais quoi' life in Paree, I adopted the Reluctant Expat philosophy: I went with my brain rather than my heart, and took the permanent job in Dubai over the freelance work in Paris. I figured that the French capital would still be there after my Arabian adventure, and perhaps there was a reason life was taking me to the Middle East.

I'm so glad that I took that one-way Emirates A380 flight to Dubai (and not just because it led to this very book deal, ahem). I probably learned more than I ever had before about myself, life, people and all those other clichés that might make you think of *Eat, Pray, Love: One Woman's Search for Everything* (or more likely Julia Roberts sweating it out in an ashram in India) during my time in The Sandpit. Life was refreshingly different. New, fun, enriching, exciting, interesting, bizarre, barmy, and brilliant all at once. A melting pot of cultures, nationalities, and lifestyles that felt magnified due to the increased interaction with people from all walks of life in a smaller city made up of around 90 percent expats. The close-knit community was a welcome change from life in London, where locals often aren't keen on eye contact, let alone conversation. I also had some of the most surreal, funniest, and memorable nights out of my life: beaches, golf buggies, car parks, you name it. Yes, even Barasti too.

I made great friends. I also met my fair share of dire Dubai expat stereotypes as well. But everyone, and every conversation I had, informed my Dubai experience. Meeting people from all over the world was one of the things I enjoyed most about living in the emirate. 'Love it or hate it,' a marketing slogan for Marmite, a British yeast-based spread, is a catchphrase that applies to Dubai like no other city on Earth (well, except maybe Las Vegas, too, I guess). Whether you love it or hate it, you can't deny that Dubai is unique and, as I hope this book suggests, the same can be said for its booming expat community.

Whether you live in Dubs, holiday there every year or have never visited in your life, I hope you'll find *Only in Dubai: An Essential Guide to the Emirate's Expats* an indispensable handbook about the people you meet. That you learn at least one thing that you didn't know before and, perhaps most importantly, that it tickles you in all the right places. As for me, it's been more than a year since I left Dubai, and I can't wait to visit. No ifs. No buts.

Sophie Robehmed,
November, 2014

The Jumeirah Janes

Once upon a time, when there weren't quite so many malls to while away the hours day in and day out, the well-to-do women living in the glamorous beachside Jumeirah 1 neighbourhood gravitated towards another haven. United by their very important (and very absent) husbands (big cheeses in aviation, business, construction and the like), these lonely ladies were one another's constant support system. They would eat together, so they didn't have to rattle around a big old villa without any adult company, and discuss strange rashes on their babies' bottoms without judgement. And so, the 'Jumeirah Jane' – a label so casually thrown around these days, most often in a derogatory manner since the JJs are a very different species now – was born from a rather special, self-named sisterhood. Bless 'em.

Not that a significant number of Dubai residents would dream of blessing the Jumeirah Janes of today, especially when they're hogging two lanes with their Range Rovers during the morning rush-hour school-run, their most strenuous activity of the day. Given their 'challenging' lifestyle, these women can generally only face Dubai traffic once a day. Naturally someone else is sent to pick up the kids in the afternoon, inevitably the maid, while the Jumeirah Jane goes about her daily rituals. These tend to revolve around the spa: lipo, Botox, skin peel, mani, pedi, full-body massage, the works. Staying beautiful, young and in tip-top shape is of the utmost importance. The JJs look immaculate 24/7 in their head-to-toe designer get-up and with their flawless skin, picture-perfect make-up, model figure, long legs up to their necks and wavy blonde hair that miraculously always stays in place, even during a sandstorm.

Daily trips to Fashion Avenue at The Dubai Mall are essential for the Jumeirah Jane, especially when the latest Peter Pilotto dress has just arrived at Bloomies. The perfect opportunity to give her hubby's credit card a workout, and leave the mall looking like a million dirhams to impress her fellow JJs at lunch somewhere equally sophisticated and stylish back in Jumeirah 1, like Comptoir 102, or the ever-faithful Limetree Café for a skin-firming smoothie. Sometimes, if the Jumeirah Janes are in the mood to talk motherhood, they'll bring their babies along, that is if they can find the time in their demanding schedules to pick them up from the maid.

After a few hours of nibbling at a salad, sipping on a juice and sharing a chocolate brownie between eight, the Jumeirah Janes bid each other adieu, driving off in the same direction, a battalion of sleek 4x4s. Exercise is next on the agenda. That means popping home to slip into the latest designer sportswear and reapplying make-up for a workout with Hot Harry, a ripped 20- or 30-something personal trainer. Just as the kids arrive home from school, she'll give a little wave as she pulls out of the driveway for the 50-metre trip to the beach to burn up a sweat (but not too much of a sweat, mind you. She wouldn't want to ruin her picture-perfect make-up).

When she can tear herself away from Hot Harry, she'll go home, shower in one of 10 bathrooms and veg out on the sofa with a gourmet meal prepared by her world-renowned nutritionist, who delivers a bespoke healthy eating programme to her every day. The kids will ask how her day was and she'll say, "Tough. I haven't stopped!" as she knocks back a shot of wheatgrass.

Most likely to say...

"Let's do lunch!"

"The nanny cancelled on me. Help!"

"Can you pick up the kids, darling? I'm stuck at the spa."

"Sometimes my kids call the maid 'Mama' by mistake. Isn't that adorable?"

"People always ask me if I miss hubby being away so much. Of course I do, but I find that a new pair of Jimmy Choos always helps to fill the void."

Popular hangouts

Tips & Toes, trying every treatment on the menu, repeatedly.

On ExpatWomen.com, venting about Spinneys' stringy avocados.

Jumeirah Beach, working on the tan 365 days a year.

The Palm Posers

"People think I'm a ponce when I say this," he said, smiling encouragingly, "but I live between Dubai and London. My dad practically invented Vodaphone." I looked down at his brick of a mobile phone. "Do you want to come back to my apartment on the Palm for an after-party?" he asked, leaning in closer. But I'd had more than enough of my fill (there was no way that I could stomach afters).

Introducing the Palm Posers, ladies and gentlemen: a supremely satisfied species, to put it politely (or, if you're the more vocal sort, you might find arrogant, pretentious and smug more fitting). Guess it's only natural that the luxury lifestyle, afforded by artificial tree-shaped islanders, will bring about this unbecoming behaviour in some Palm Posers. Perhaps it's a blessing in disguise that no one currently lives on any of the World Islands.

Not all Palm Posers are jet-setting playboys with practically obsolete mobile phones, however. Palm living is popular with oil and gas employees, engineers, bankers, businessmen, doctors, the *crème de la crème* of the media world, high-flying lawyers – basically any man or woman who is earning the big dirhams. Nor are all Palm Posers up their own backsides, either. But what all Palm Posers share, regardless of their profession or persona, is an overwhelming sense of pride that they live on this self-proclaimed eighth wonder of the world, an artificial archipelago that is bigger, bolder and brasher than 800 football fields. After all, not many people can say that they live on a palm tree-shaped island, can they? Few folks will be able to regale the grandkids with the sun-kissed days spent in a blinged-out villa on one of the 17 fronds or, even better, a swish apartment on the Palm's one and only trunk.

Needless to say, Palm Posers are loyal to the hilt when it comes to their island. It's OK for them to utter Palm-living pet peeves among themselves, but should any outsiders express even mild irritation over the excessive speed bumps, elite beach club membership schemes, or how the island lacks 'community', prepare for nuclear warfare. Or a lengthy lecture on why your outlook is all wrong, and the Palm is the greatest invention since denim.

When the Palm Poser – a keen social butterfly – is not in any number of high-profile establishments on the island (brunching at Saffron, lunching at Nobu or singing the night away at MusicHall), you are guaranteed to spot at least one zooming down the Sheikh Zayed Road in an Aston Martin, Ferrari or Lamborghini. Many Palm Posers enjoy nothing more than parking their flash wheels outside the Mall of the Emirates so that they can be admired by one and all.

But while the mall offers the Palm Posers the opportunity to shop to their lavish hearts' content, the unfortunate hordes of shoppers, noise pollution and subsequent soaring stress levels chipping away at their 'island state of mind' leads to a mental meltdown every time they visit. Before you can say 'Palm Jumeirah', the Palm Posers are zooming towards Exit 35 on the Sheikh Zayed Road, returning to their beloved paradise as quickly as possible.

Most likely to say...

"Speed bumps, schpeed bumps! Have you seen the view from my balcony, sweetheart? Well worth the Dhs4,950,000 price tag alone, believe me."

"I wouldn't trade the life I have on the Palm for New York, London, Paris or Rome. I'm sorry but none of those cities can ever come close to a palm tree-shaped island. End of story."

"When I die, I want my ashes to be sprinkled at the top of the Leap of Faith waterslide at Aquaventure - you know, that water park at Atlantis the Palm? - because living here is the biggest and best ride of my life."

Popular hangouts

RIVA Beach Resort, hogging the sun loungers, especially on weekends.

West 14th in Oceana Beach Club, scoffing a steak and frites and washing it down with the most expensive bubbles available.

The Jumeirah Zabeel Saray, swanning around in designer threads.

The Media City Moguls

One thing that you might not know about Dubai, dear reader, is that it's quite possibly the most literal city in the world. To give you an idea, there's Healthcare City (where, unsurprisingly enough, you'll find two hospitals and more than 120 medical centres), Internet City (where, drum roll... global technology companies reside), Knowledge Village (a personal favourite: where students flock to stretch their grey matter at several academic institutions) and Media City (where, you guessed it, most of the biggest and best media companies are based).

For the Media City Mogul, these eponymous streets are, quite simply, the *raison d'être*. The very reason why many career-hungry journalists, designers, film-makers, photographers, and PR specialists up sticks from their native Australia, Blighty, Canada, India, Lebanon, New Zealand, South Africa, USA, and so on, for the opportunity to accelerate their careers. And to work in a media bubble where the word 'recession' is replaced with 'regular perks' like free manis, pedis and massages in the canteen (for those who can squeeze it into their schedule), designer hampers, and press tickets to every event happening at that patch of grass opposite the CNN building. While the daily freebies are warmly received, it doesn't take long for the Mogul on smaller teams (saddled with the equivalent of five people's jobs back home) to learn that Media City life is work-hard and hopefully play-when-you're-lucky-enough-to-leave-the-office-before-everyone-leaves-that-launch-you-were-invited-to.

Caffeine is the Mogul's best and most trusted friend. A vital elixir of life. So much so that no distance is too far for that precious espresso, diet coke fix, or even just a slice of that unforgettable carrot cake, not even the trek across the car park to the Lime Tree Café & Kitchen in the scorching midday heat. That is, if the Mogul can actually escape work longer than the time it takes to ask the barista in the tea room if he'd kindly inject caffeine straight into his or her veins. For the Mogul drowning in deadlines, the endless possibilities for a breakfast, lunch and dinner delivery is the silver lining amid the constant eyestrain, tear-inducing neck spasms and shakes from a caffeine overdose.

Thankfully, a totally work-free weekend is a welcome treat for even the most overworked Moguls, who generally try to stay as far away as possible from Media City, which is tricky for many of them who live in neighbouring Dubai Marina. Not that it matters, of course. Before you know it, it's Sunday again and the never-ending cycle of deadlines, RSI and takeaway conundrums begin again.

But at least these stressed-out souls can endeavour to walk to Media City's very own lake at least one working day a week, to gaze longingly at the ducks, roaming free, and get a much-needed reality check on their work-life balance. Either that, or they can dive right in and return to the office dripping wet, wide-eyed and wild, having lost it once and for all.

Most likely to tweet...

"Had to miss work as I couldn't lift my own head out of bed. (Muscle spasm. Disc pressing on nerve.) Body now pumped with Tramadol. OH, YES."

"It might have been another 14-hour day, and it might be midnight. But surviving another week + freedom for 57 hours = PARTY!"

"Did everyone enjoy the launch party last night? It was absolutely amazing. OK, the photos looked absolutely amazing. I was at work. #quelsurpris #storyofmylife"

Popular hangouts

The Magazine Shop, to pick up the latest issue of a terribly hip magazine from Outer Mongolia.

On the phone to Circle Café, ordering enough food to stave off hunger until leaving the office in the early hours.

The Sushi Counter, getting that all-important raw fish fix in a bid to fight the desk-bound bulge.

The Taxi Drivers

Ah, the Taxi Driver's life isn't easy to navigate, nor are the city's largely unnamed roads come to think of it. But perhaps the Taxi Driver should learn not to rub his passengers the wrong way with the usual cross-examination. No three questions, however, are more pertinent to a Taxi Driver in Dubai than:

1. "Where are you from?" (OK, we can give them that one considering everyone asks you that in this city.)
2. "How old are you?" (Why is this relevant to our light chit-chat?)
3. And – the *pièce de résistance* – "Are you married?"

Long-term expats, and perhaps even concerned parents at home, will tell you to wear a wedding ring even if you're not married, or to make up an elaborate story about your hubby, two kids, and corpulent tabby, Chahna, because it's "the easiest way". They are probably right. The alternative, you see, is being bombarded with an in-depth analysis of philosophically grandiose proportions as to why you're not married yet (apparently late twenties makes you ancient). This is traditionally followed by the legendary 'importance of marriage' lecture. The thought that maybe you would be married if you'd found the right person never seems to arise.

Then come the speed-fire question rounds that, believe it or

The Taxi Drivers

not, are even more personal than the first ones. Fine examples of this tactful approach include, "What's your salary?" followed by, "Why won't you tell me? I will find out." You make a speedy exit, hoping you'll never have to sit in the backseat of that car ever again, while being fully aware that you probably will because, unless you own a car, you are condemned to spending 99.9 percent of your time travelling by taxi. All I'm saying, based on personal experience, is don't be surprised if you happen to hop into that intrusive taxi driver's car again after a long day at work, at which point he will laugh manically like Jack Nicholson in *The Shining* all the way home.

The standard Taxi Driver is male, and generally hails from Bangladesh, Pakistan, Sri Lanka, Nepal, India, or elsewhere from the South Asian subcontinent. His hair tends to be slicked back and his car usually smells of fake evergreen trees mixed with Dhs10 aftershave so strong that you'll forget what fresh air is, or body odour so potent that it will make you gag. The last one is particularly unfortunate, especially in the summer when temperatures soar into the high 40s, sometimes low 50s. Sure, you can casually open those windows and let that sizzling heat right in, but good luck with that.

But, if you truly are in luck, you will come across a rare breed of Taxi Driver – the Lady Taxi Driver – and have a stress-free, sweet-smelling, downright pleasant journey. Sadly, that's only if you book a Lady Taxi Driver on purpose, or happen to flag her down on her way to and from the airport, mind you. So, best prepare yourself for an interrogation, and the most nail-biting ride of your life in the face of unwanted questions, aromas and a potential head-on collision.

Most likely to ask...

"Any children?"

"But, why aren't you married?"

"Ever been to Pakistan?"

"What do you do? Good job? Good money?"

"You like Dubai?"

"How long have you lived here?"

Popular hangouts

The Sheikh Zayed Road, swerving between lanes like a ninja with super powers.

Choithrams in Deira, stocking up on the three essentials: bottled water, evergreen tree air fresheners and aftershave.

Resting a weary head on the wheel, catching some Z's in between shifts.

The Yo-Yo Dieters

For the emirate's contingent of Yo-Yo Dieters, the city of takeaways, taxis and short-lived pavements are a constant burden to their weight woes. And that, my friends, is because not long after any expat has touched down in The Sandpit, someone utters two words that will change their lives forever: "Dubai stone".

If you're wondering how a rock could prove so problematic, the Dubai stone is in fact a reference to how all expats apparently balloon within the first six months of their arrival. While its weighty promise hangs ominously over newbies' heads, most take it in their stride, brunching in moderation, walking where possible and making it to the gym occasionally. But for the Yo-Yo Dieters, the Dubai stone is a constant battle against another inviting profiterole, unfortunate personal training injuries ("Just a touch of coccydynia again!"), extreme self-loathing and experimenting with every bizarre diet that they can think of, or cook up.

It doesn't take long to recognise a Yo-Yo Dieter. Within the first couple minutes of a conversation, there is usually a reference to "This new diet I'm on", which is simply "All the rage! Its roots lie in what tribal people eat in Amazonian jungles", or, "I might look a state but I was paddleboarding at 6am and my face shows just how intense that workout was" or even, "Would you mind rubbing some Deep Heat into my lower buttocks? I can't quite reach." It is moments like these when the Yo-Yo

Dieters are happiest, despite the fact that they might look a wreck, their stomachs might rattle at every work lunch, and they might hobble around in acute agony. These, believe it or not, are the moments that the Yo-Yo Dieters thrive upon, convinced that they are finally on their way to a lithe life. That their idea of perfection, based upon the pictures of beautiful women with toned tums and athletic men with bulging biceps that they've stuck on their wardrobes, is in sight. (Or at least one-sixteenth of the way there.)

The Yo-Yo Dieters' 'perfect body' expectations might be sized up as delusional at times but, deep down, they know they are only one Friday away from an excessive brunch, a mid-week Burger Fuel delivery and a skipped pre-work pilates-cum-pole-dancing-cum-power-walking session. And when that happens, it's one slippery slope towards reviving their co-dependent relationship with taxis, and catching a ride to the end of the street for a pint of (skimmed) milk.

The fate of the Yo-Yo Dieters lies in the balance. They either continue that uphill struggle, fighting the bulge with every fibre of their being (and perhaps even becoming a Dubai stone success story in *Gulf News' Friday* magazine in the process). Or they give in to the endless temptation that surrounds them, lose the ability to walk up a few stairs, and accept the crushing reality that they'll never look remotely like anyone in the posters on their wardrobes. Either way, they'll never feel like their load has been lightened, but such is the life of a Yo-Yo Dieter.

Most likely to say...

"I'm on the 'BB' diet. I blink more than usual to speed up calorie burning, and I just eat bananas."

"I'm having trouble walking but I feel so alive right now. Man, that techno skating-pilates-trapeze-trampoline session was just what I needed."

"Every time a square of chocolate passes my lips, my thighs shake. I think it's my body's way of telling me, 'Nooooo!'"

Popular hangouts

Tribefit, attending every event going on.

In the physiotherapy waiting room at the Saudi German Hospital, preparing to work through 'muscle issues'.

Browsing kcalhealthyfastfood.com for another well-balanced takeaway.

The Bling Bloggers

Following a lavish gala dinner in Paris, overlooking the Eiffel Tower on the first evening of a press trip, a Bling Blogger turned to me and said, "This trip feels very low-budget." Apparently, being flown to one of the most beautiful cities in the world + flying with Emirates (one of the best airlines in the world) = nil point.

And that's because the Bling Bloggers don't, under 'normal' circumstances, 'do' economy travel ("How is one suppose to blog with such limited arm space?"). Nor, seemingly, do they waste any of their precious time waiting to be driven wherever they need to go. Naturally, dahlings – they're the Bling Bloggers!

These tweenies and 20-somethings tend to be over-indulged Third Culture Kids (see page 60) who consider themselves Dubai aristocracy. Their wardrobes are kitted out with the latest offerings from big-name designers fresh off the catwalks of New York, London, Paris and Milan. Sometimes, because they know somebody, these privileged, bright young things even get a preview sample dress from a major designer (or, failing that, the new Middle Eastern name *du jour*) to flaunt at every showbiz party.

Day and night, the Bling Bloggers' diaries are crammed with high-profile business meetings all over Internet City and via Skype, with global web, picture and video-sharing companies promising blogging stardom, and six-figure advances when their blog gets turned into a book. Social engagements take precedence for the Bling Bloggers, too: whether it's a 10-course dinner at the Burj Khalifa for the region's best bloggers, a hand care convention guiding bloggers on how to keep their hands in tip-top condition or, if the BBs get really desperate for self-promotion, even cutting the banner at the launch of a hair salon in Satwa.

But generally the Bling Bloggers have to make time in their already jam-packed itineraries to arrange their diaries because they are so very, very, *very* busy. Taking time out to organise their lives is, of course, an added strain that leads them to curse the need to sleep, eat, empty their bowels, take a dip in the pool, have a massage, shower, pedicure, manicure, tweet a link on the shifting media landscape to sound intelligent, Instagram lunch, write a blog post that reads like an advertorial to keep sponsors happy… the list is endless.

While the Bling Bloggers resent life getting in the way, keeping their bodies fit and their minds happy is crucial. It's what keeps them at the heart of the world's blogging elite until the day internet domination is theirs, all theirs, or until carpel tunnel claims their worn-out fingers and thumbs.

Most likely to blog...

"Sometimes it's really hard being a blogger. You've got to make some serious sacrifices - my family and friends don't see me as much as they'd like, looking this perfect all the time is both mentally and physically draining, and I've had to rent another villa to store all my freebies. But I wouldn't have it any other way. I feel blessed to be who I am and I know you, dear readers, feel blessed to have me in your lives, too.

So, what I'm really trying to say is: don't ever give up on your DREAMS. One day, you might be a blogger like me, too. But don't worry if it never happens for you, it just means that it was never your destiny. Mwah!"

Popular hangouts

MAKE Business Hub, looking lost in deep thought with a MacBook Pro and latte.

The technology pages of every publication going in every corner of the Gulf, offering readers 'blogging advice'. (A crucial element of the self-promotion strategy.)

Sitting in the back seat of a stretch limousine in Internet City en route to very important meetings with Facebook, Google, Microsoft et al.

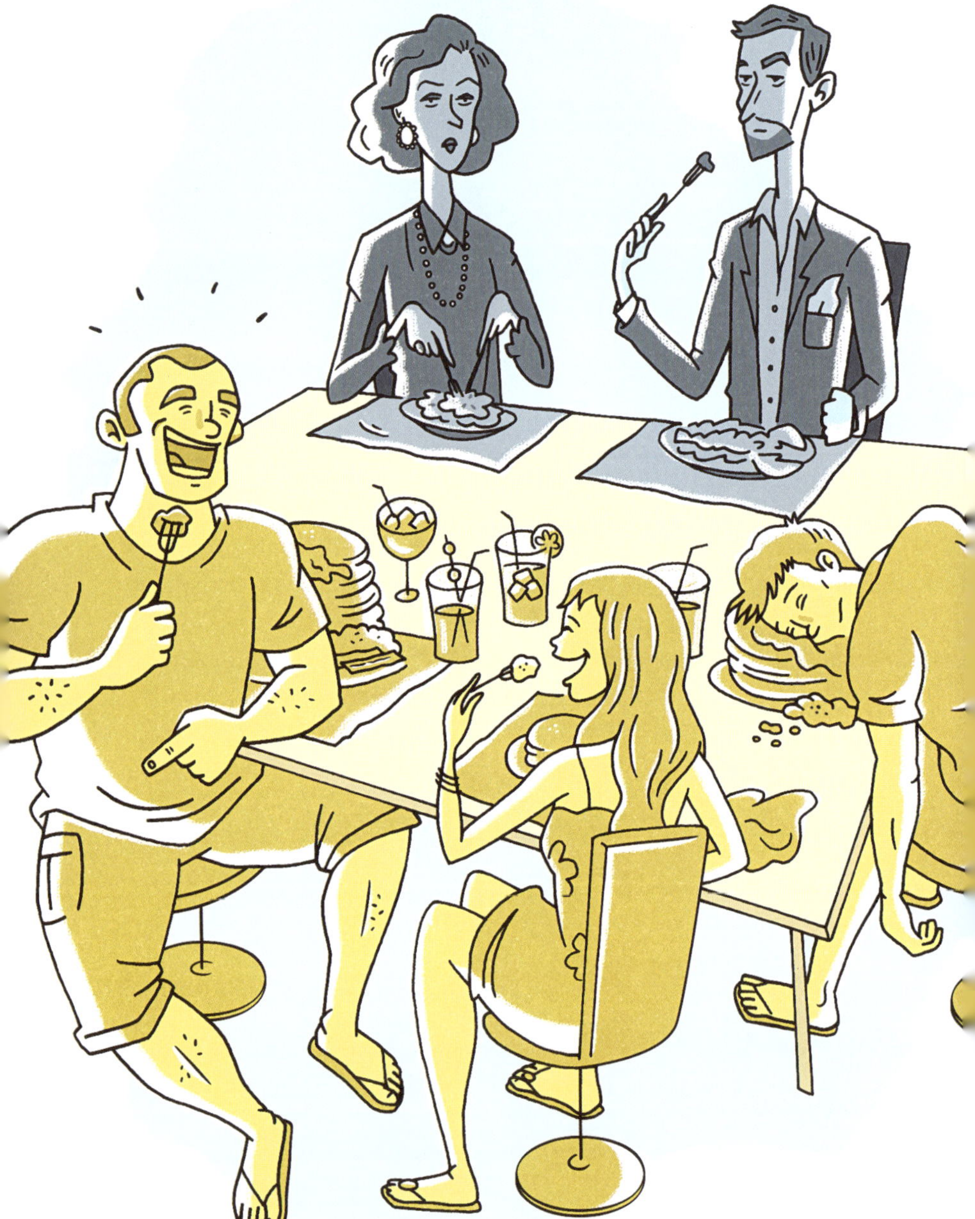

The Brunch Brits

The British are great sticklers for tradition. Most Brits couldn't go a day without at least one cup of tea. Eating fish and chips out of soggy newspaper by the sea is a popular pastime, even if it's lashing down with rain. And, speaking of precipitation, no one can talk about the weather like the British, probably because dear ol' Blighty is possibly the only place in the world where you can enjoy all four seasons in one day. So it's hardly surprising that the Brunch Brits grab Dubai's Friday late-morning-cum-early-afternoon dining tradition by the horns.

Now, I know what you're thinking, but not all Brunch Brits end up burnt to a crisp and lying in a paddling pool with a thumping head almost as soon as they've sat down to dine the day away. And that's because the Brunch Brits are split into two polar opposite sub-categories: the Over-indulgers and the Traditionalists.

The Over-indulgers aren't at all fussy about where they eat and drink. All they care about is just how much food and bubbles they can get for as few dirhams as possible, every Friday, without fail. The Traditionalists, on the other hand, most certainly do not brunch every week. Many, if not most, avoid it like the plague. It's a waste of money, it takes too long, and they don't want to eat and drink until they need to be airlifted to their beds. But what they truly dread is bumping into those lairy Over-indulgers. They will bite the bullet and keep a stiff upper lip if a brunch is a special occasion for someone they genuinely love. They do, more often than not, end up having a jolly good knees-up, surprised at the extent to which they enjoyed the fine food, a vintage drink or two, the odd atmospheric panpipes, and the opportunity to catch up with loved ones and friends.

If you're new to the Dubai brunching scene, don't fret. You'll work it out. You'll know instinctively whether you're an Over-indulger or Traditionalist, and should similarly be able to determine which side hosts support depending on how they conduct themselves, their general demeanour, and their choice of venue. Just make sure you've mentally prepared your RSVP response the next time someone puts you on the spot with a "Let's do brunch!" And remember: a cup of tea solves everything, even brunching against your will. That's the spirit! Oh, and for the Over-indulgers reading this who are sick of the Traditionalists being such dullards, here are a few words that shouldn't get lost in translation: brunch at Warehouse. Friday. Living it large in Garhoud. Yes, mate. Wheyyyy!

Most likely Facebook status from...

The Over-indulgers
"Worst week everrrr!!!! Can't wait to get my brunch on at the Irish Village!! Been starving myself this week so I'm ready for this. Lol, gonna be messy!!!!"

The Traditionalists
"There's nothing I dread more than an eight-course degustation, even if it is at The Ivy. Please. Save. Me. (Sorry, hubby, I love you really. Happy 40th birthday!)"

Popular hangouts

For the Over-indulgers...
McGettigan's in Jumeirah Lake Towers, lapping up a fry-up and exceeding the three house drinks included in the Dhs129 brunch deal within thirty minutes. They'll naturally be cursing the fact that they're not getting rowdy downtown at Double Decker with their fellow flirty, fun, party-loving Brits.

For the Traditionalists...
Traiteur at Park Hyatt Dubai, munching on lobster while soaking up Beethoven and mentally buying all the yachts in the harbour.

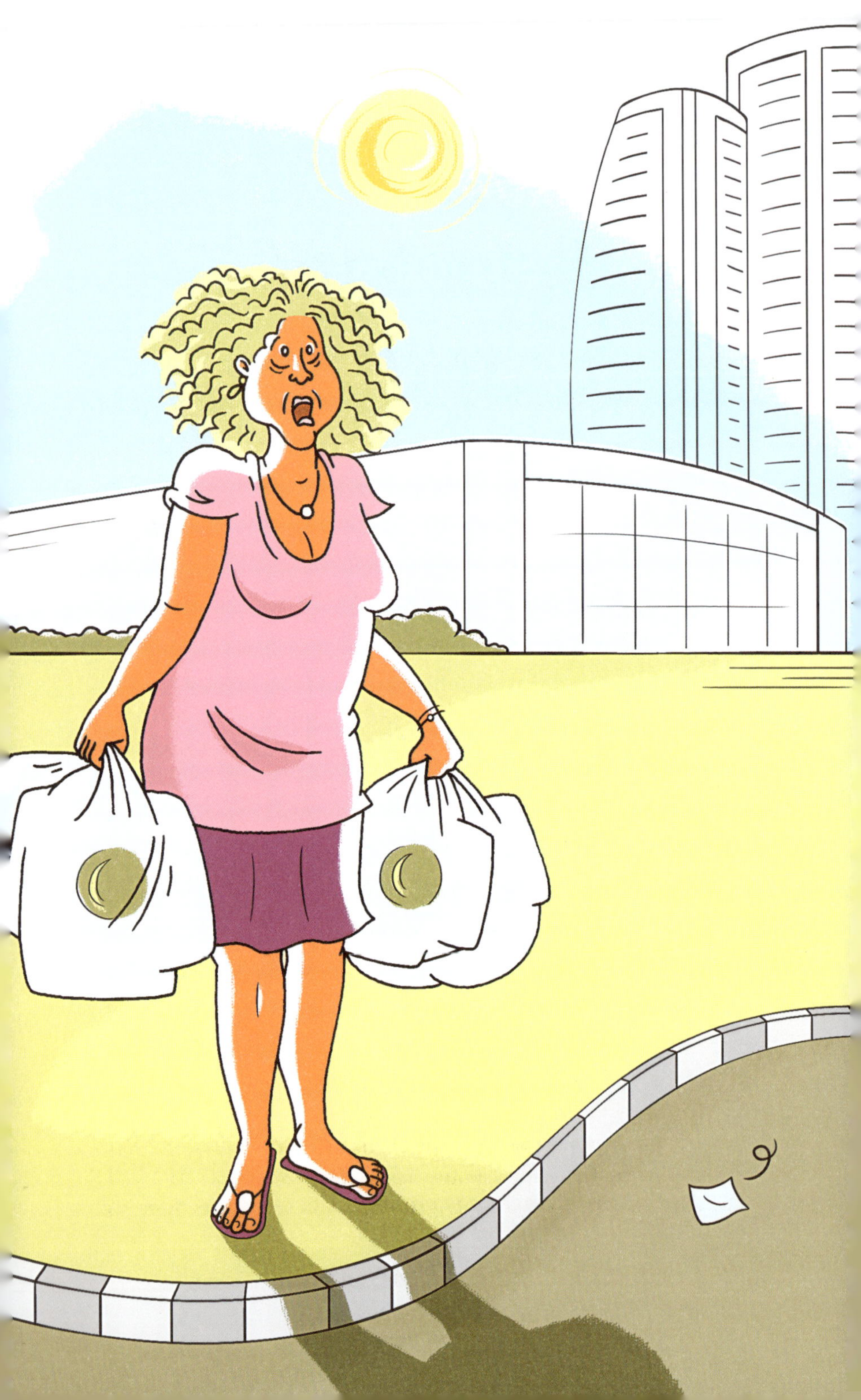

The Reluctant Expats

*A*ll Reluctant Expats have a well-rehearsed explanation as to why Dubai is not the city for them. A justification they inexplicably feel compelled to repeat to anyone and everyone who will listen. You'll wonder why they don't just buy a one-way ticket out of town already if the city is grating on them that much?! But the Reluctant Expats know that if they did that, they'd miss filling all the natural silences of a conversation with something they couldn't say at home with so much satisfaction: "Another thing that doesn't make sense about this city is…"

You'll know if you've met a Reluctant Expat almost immediately. And if you haven't had the pleasure of crossing paths with one just yet, you can look forward to an enlightening conversation, full of hope, positivity and light, similar to the following fictitious interaction:

You: Great to meet you. I see from our records that you haven't been in Dubai very long, so welcome!

Reluctant Expat (RE): Oh, thanks. But you might be wasting your breath.

You: I'm sorry?

RE: Yeah, I don't think it's for me. I never even wanted to visit Dubai, let alone live here. I know, it's pretty funny, isn't it? I had my heart set on Paris, not Dubai, but the job was better here so I went with my brain instead.

You: Oh… Maybe Dubai will grow on you. Happens to a lot of…

RE: No, I don't think so. It's just not very me, y'know. I'm not very materialistic, or into malls. I crave culture.
You: Oh, well there's loads of culture here. I imagine you might have read that Dubai is shallow, just shopping, glitz and glamour. But you only have to go to the desert, Dubai Creek or Alserkal Avenue to find…
RE: Then there's the labourers who work such long hours in the scorching heat for peanuts. I am fed up of hearing people justify their reality by saying that they are better off here than they would be in their own countries. It just doesn't sit right with me, y'know? It is far too hot here, and I want to open the windows at work but no, we mustn't because "it will affect the air-con". I don't want to waste my life breathing in recycled air.
You: I see… Whereabouts are you living?
RE: Dubai Marina.
You: That's nice, especially for a newbie. One of the best expat communities.
RE: *So. Noisy.* I'm barely sleeping. I've actually become a nanosecond sleeper for the first time in my life – I've lost count of the times that I've head-butted the computer screen at work. I fell asleep on a biro the other day. The pen shot so far up my nose that I'm lucky it didn't impale my brain. The traffic is terrible. These days, I give up waiting for a taxi at that pitiful roundabout near Spinneys, and end up struggling back home with the weekly shop on foot. Of course, I have to jump straight into the shower when I do that, because I'm so disgustingly sweaty. And why is there still so much construction everywhere? We're paying so much money to live in an area surrounded by cement, it's ridiculous.
You: Well, it's been lovely meeting you, but I see that quite a queue has built up since we've been chatting. If you'd like to take a seat, the bank manager will be out to meet you in no time at all.
RE: Pah, I'll believe that when I see it! Everything takes so long around here. I'll probably be dead by the time our meeting starts.
 A lot of Reluctant Expats give Dubai life six months, if that.

In the days running up to their departure, sadness creeps in – they will, believe it or not, miss the handful of friends that stood by them, the novel luxury of getting a taxi everywhere they go, and even their pharmacist, Kareem, who helped them more than any sleeping tablet ever did. He or she will well up as the plane lifts off the tarmac at Dubai International Airport, and give the Burj Khalifa a little teary wave from the window seat, before turning to the passenger on the right, saying, "I used to live in Dubai. Interesting place, but not for me."

Most likely to vent...

"Some people are just not Dubai people, y'know what I mean?"

"Do you remember when JLo sang that song about 'being real'? I listen to that song on repeat now, and crank it up on my balcony to teach the people of this city what sincerity means."

"I've only been to The Dubai Mall. And frankly, that was enough for me. I don't give two flying figs if it's the biggest shopping centre in the world. Give me a high street with shops any day."

Popular hangouts

Carrefour in the Mall of the Emirates, stocking up on every familiar brand.

In bed, streaming their favourite shows online because they're not available on any television packages in Dubai. (Of course they aren't.)

On the phone to Du, asking to maximise the number of minutes to phone numbers back home.

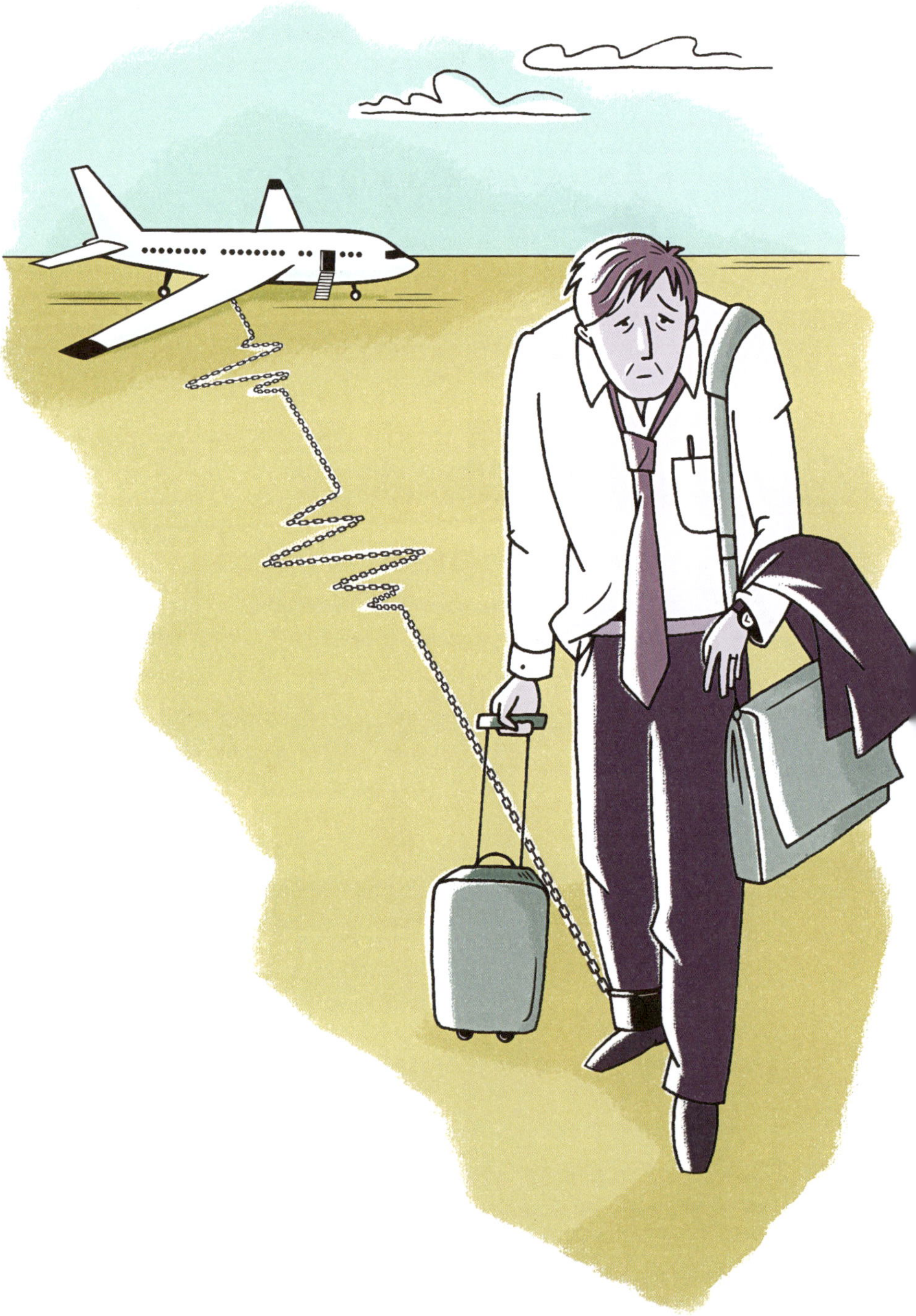

The Transients

"Unpack and repack!"
"And it starts again… packing"
"Heading to my second home… Emirates!"

My cousin, Fady, the most extreme Transient I knew in Dubai, would share his constant comings and goings with his friends. A seemingly never-ending stream of geographical updates naturally featured on Facebook: Cairo – at airport – Chicago – Orlando – New York – Dubai – Jeddah – Cairo – Lebanon – Riyadh – Dubai – Lebanon – Tunisia – Dubai – Beirut – Dubai – Paris – airport again!!!! – Paris – Dubai…

Transient is a word that is often thrown about, or insinuated, when discussing Dubai:

"Oh, Dubai's so transient, everyone's always coming and going."

"The turnover is so high at work. There's always a new face in the office."

"It's hard when friends leave, but the constant goodbyes are just a part of life here."

Truth is, unless you're a national, there comes a time when everyone leaves. And you quickly learn of your friends' intentions. You know the ones that will stay for up to five years, the ones who told you they had a two-year plan and show no signs of budging three years later, and the ones who feel more at home in Dubai than where they came from, and would never dream of putting a time limit on their life in the emirate.

But then there are the Transients, who are continuously coming and going during their time in Dubai, so much so it's as if they're never really around at all. Any given Transient might have technically been living in Dubai for two years but never even made it to the beach to feel the warm waves crash against their weary, well-travelled bodies. And that's because the Transient is a slave to his or her work, predominantly high-powered business folk, with a demanding itinerary of appointments, conferences and visits scheduled around the Middle East, Africa, Europe and beyond.

The Transients often won't know when they're going away, or where they are being sent, until the very last minute. This makes having a social life tremendously tricky. Those with wives (see the Jumeirah Janes on page 12) or husbands, and children, might find themselves staring wistfully at a family portrait on their mobile phones, somewhere over the Atlantic, with no idea what time it is in Dubai, and whether their families are awake or asleep. While the Transients might not spend nearly enough time with their loved ones or besties, they are in a very intimate relationship with jet lag. Spending nearly all their life in the air, jumping time zones as often as the sun shines in Dubai, their very notion of time has blurred. They're in an airborne twilight zone, where they don't know whether the plate of food they just polished off counts as breakfast, lunch or dinner, or whether their name is in fact Michael or Michelle.

And yet, even through the fog of jet lag, they never have any problem recognising the arrivals hall at Dubai International Airport. Sometimes, as they drag their throbbing feet through Arrivals, they realise that there is little point in going home before their next flight. Heading to Departures instead, an existential crisis hits. The Transients worry that the airport is starting to feel more like home than their Dubai home or even their home-home, and whether they are turning into Tom Hanks's character in *The Terminal*. But at least they can always soothe their frazzled minds with a shopping spree to fuel the steady supply of 'Sorry I never see you' gifts for family and friends, bought with their umpteen air miles. After all, every cloud has a silver lining. All of them. And life is always full of gates to new journeys. The Transients know all about that.

Most likely to email...

From: Ispendmylifeintransit@sure.com
To: MyJumeirahJanewife@livid.com
Subject: RE: My present!
Date: Wed, 28 May 2014 00:04:49 +0000

I'm in the Hatton Garden jewellery quarter in London, darling. Was it just a pink diamond earring-necklace-bracelet-anklet set that you were after?

From: Ihavenosociallife@shame.com
To: Mybestmate@tickedoff.com
Subject: RE: Birthday drinks
Date: Fri, 30 May 2014 02:12:33 +0000

Sorry to say I won't be making your birthday drinks tomorrow after all. Just found out that I won't be able to get back from Singapore in time. Maybe next year?

Popular hangouts

Shake Shack in Terminal 3 at Dubai International Airport, on a comfort-eating burger binge.

In the shower, using up all the cold water at Dubai International Airport Hotel in an attempt to wake up in between flights.

Writing another new life plan at 35,000 feet, triggered by an in-flight curry that tasted like chilli con carne, with baby twins crying in unison as background music, and the hallucinatory clarity of five hours sleep in the last 48 hours.

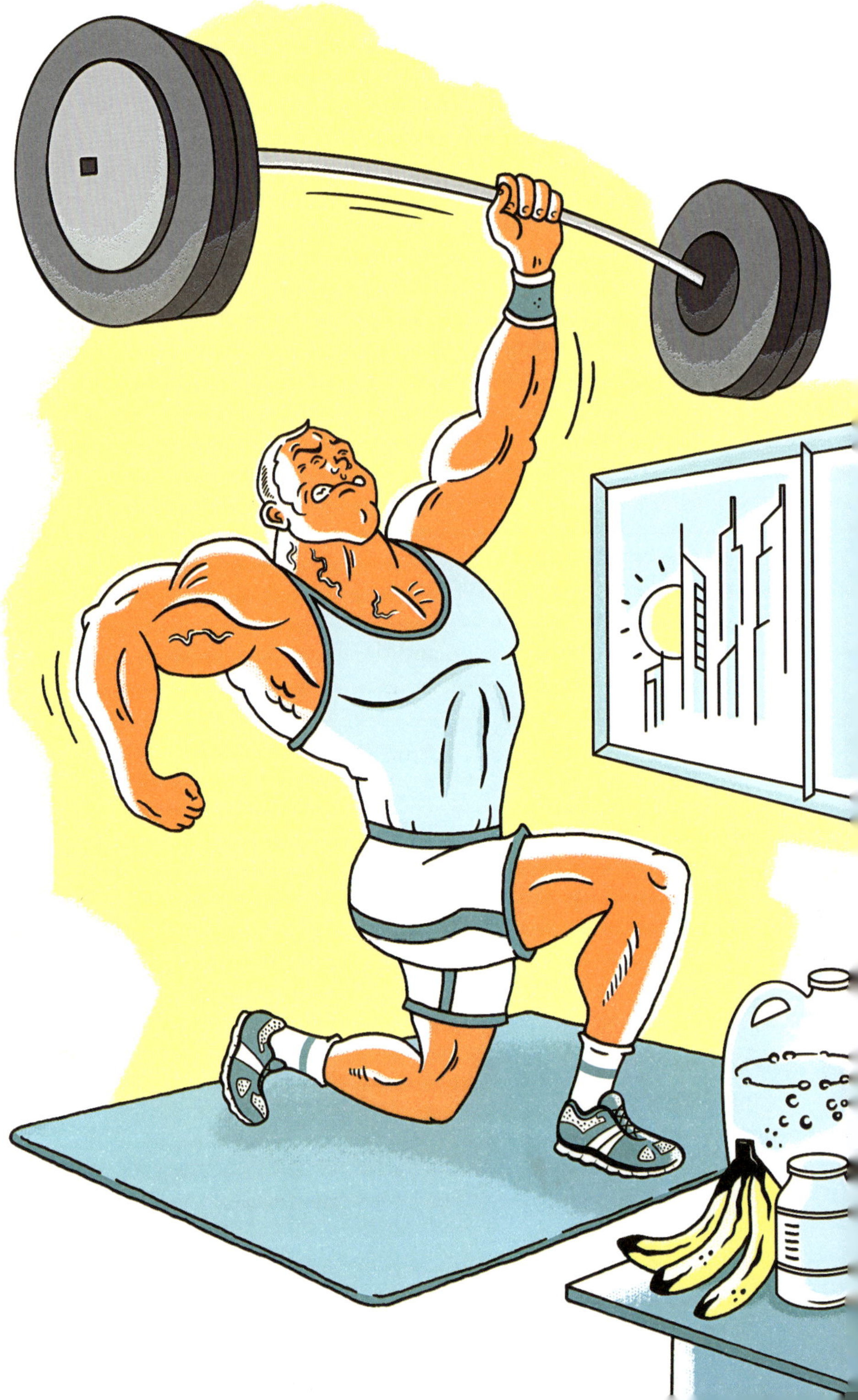

The Gym Obsessives

While the majority of Dubai's expats shy away from regular trips to the gym, even though they are conveniently located in their apartment blocks, the Gym Obsessives can't get enough of this sweaty, smelly and stark sanctuary. The Gym Obsessives are the first and last visitors, itching to get a mega dose of HIIT (that's some sort of interval cardio to you and me) at dawn and the last to leave the elliptical trainer at night, but only because the security guard is hot on his or her heels to lock up shop.

And you can bet your lycra shorts that a Gym Obsessive will manage to sneak in a "cheeky sesh" right in the middle of the working day, followed by a lean turkey steak with a side dish of wilted spinach before a triumphant return to the office to bore colleagues about the five sets of 100lb weights "for gainz". In case you're perplexed by the lingo Gym Obsessives casually drop in everyday conversations, urbandictionary.com sums up 'gainz' pretty nicely: "What you get from curling in the squat rack and dumbbell pressing every day". (Here's hoping you gain something from this newfound knowledge.) To be honest, as long as you're *au fait* with 'gainz', 'reps' (the number of times they do a particular exercise, which, you'll soon gather, they find inordinately impressive) and can tolerate being called 'bro' as a term of endearment regardless of whether you're a man or a woman, then you'll get by.

When the Gym Obsessives aren't at the gym, they are

thinking about going to the gym, and talking about going to the gym, even if there is no one there to listen to them. Those Gym Obsessives who aren't personal trainers, professional weight lifters, P.E. teachers or the like, constantly dream of quitting the nine-to-five shackles for something sporty that could pay them as well as their sales manager jobs do. That way, they might spend every waking hour at the gym and stop themselves feeling like a battery chicken, cooped up, bored and sedentary at their work station.

The Gym Obsessives are a restless gang and rush to find creative channels for their excessive energy. This is why it's not uncommon to see them lifting their computer monitors above their heads while at work, something that their colleagues soon learn to ignore. Naturally, the office, limited pavements and malls become the Gym Obsessives' surrogate playgrounds during the hours that they cannot be at their sweaty sanctuary, bench pressing 1,000 kilos and doing back-to-back Zumba classes. Pedestrians climb over Gym Obsessives, who have fallen to the floor to do five reps of 20 push-ups in the mid-afternoon sun. Shoppers, meanwhile, shout words of encouragement whenever they spot Gym Obsessives running around, and over, people in The Dubai Mall, as if it's the world's biggest obstacle course.

Despite any frustrations brought on from gym withdrawal throughout the working day, Gym Obsessives are a well-groomed, vain but amiable bunch on the whole, content with life as long as they can see that the sun is shining from the gym, they're making gainz, and no one is hogging the weights.

Most likely to boast...

"I placed my upper arms on the kitchen scales the other day and they broke under the weight of my gainz! I am unstoppable."

"Sometimes, when I'm running so fast on the treadmill, I swear I can feel the weight sliding off me. I can't be imagining it, though, as I've already been awarded six grams in gold for losing three kilos. I'm on fire."

"I'm not one to big myself up, but my body is probably the buffest it ever has been right now. It's a body that should be applauded _ I've worked my butt off to get here, and eaten my weight in steak 10 times over."

Popular hangouts

Carrefour in the Mall of the Emirates, stocking up on an array of Maximuscle protein shake powders.

Sweatshop Studios in Jumeirah Lake Towers, trying, but failing, to get into Moksha yoga. Sorry, Yogis (see p 80), it doesn't even come close.

Standing at the foot of the Burj Khalifa, checking out how big their muscles look in the reflection.

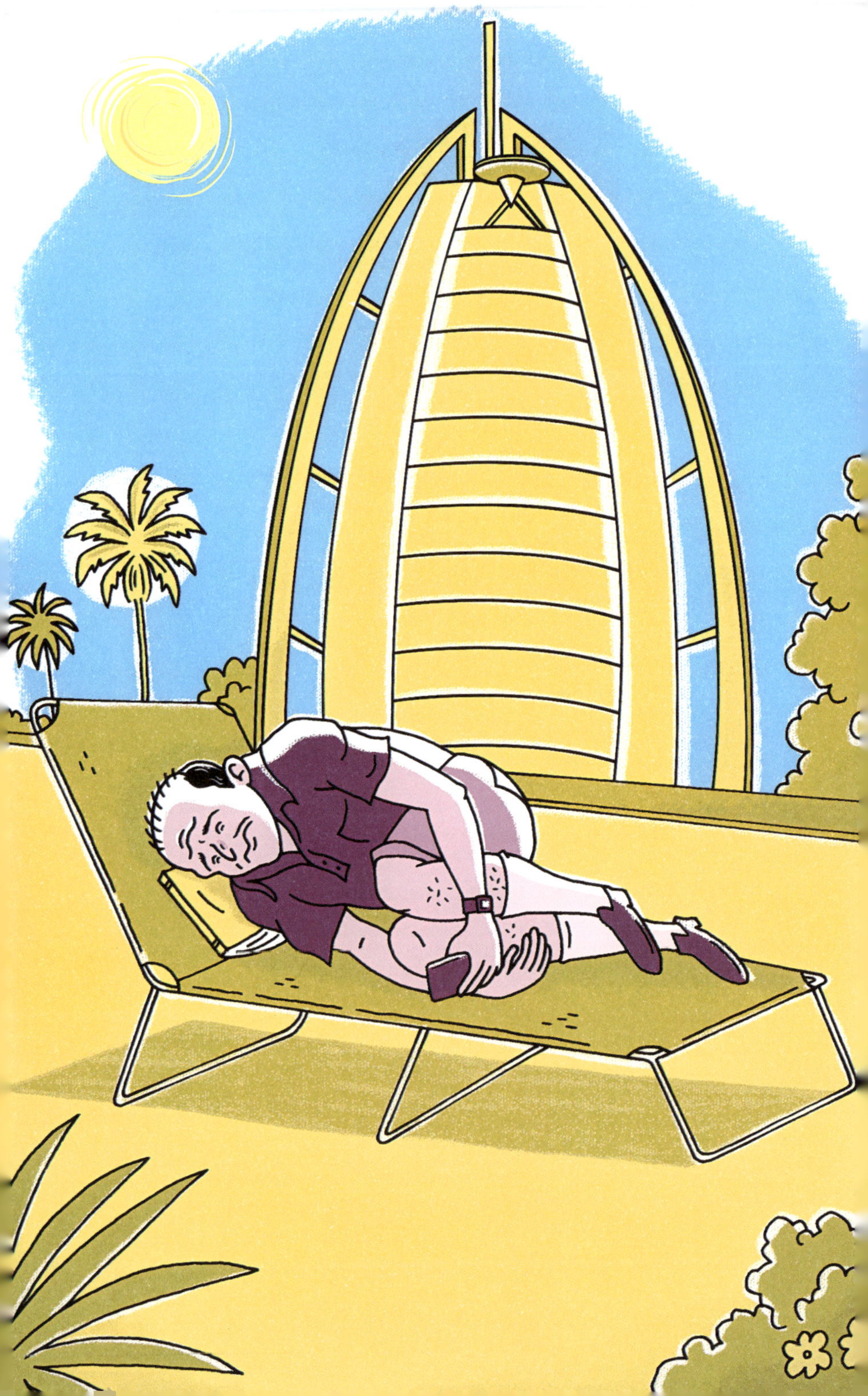

The Lost Souls

Ah, Dubai! A melting pot of nationalities, cultures, and outlooks that also happens to be bursting at the seams with the Lost Souls. Believe me, no other city re-homes the recently divorced, the newly single, the disillusioned, the quarter/mid/late-life crisis-stricken, like this city. It doesn't matter whether you've been in the emirate five minutes or five years, you're guaranteed to meet at least one Lost Soul on a daily, weekly or monthly basis.

The Lost Souls open up to new people like no other expat. Their response to the inevitable question, "Why did you move to Dubai?" is most often what gives their disguise away. That's when it all spills out, comes to a head – just like their recent break-up.

"I split up with my boyfriend."

"Oh, I'm sorry to hear that. When was that?"

"Two months ago." TWO MONTHS AGO!

"And so you thought you'd just move to Dubai?"

"Yep, something like that. Why not, eh? I'd always wanted to work abroad, and this seemed like the best time to do it – before I actually meet the love of my life and end up going nowhere."

Following such a conversation, don't be surprised if you then witness said Lost Soul sat at a table and surrounded by a bevy of potential suitors.

It's not unusual to have just met a Lost Soul for the first time and for him or her to tell you everything about everything: what happened before they left home, what they hope to achieve from this drastic life change, and even what they made of the moutabel they had with their flatbread 30 seconds ago because they've never had hummus with aubergine before. Such is their need to talk to someone, anyone, about every incident leading up to their Dubai move, in addition to every fleeting thought or encounter since then. As first meetings go, it might be a little draining and incredibly intense, but lend a caring ear and be thankful that you can walk away. After all, the Lost Souls cannot escape their countless uncertainties, contradictory motives for moving to the emirate, and the unsettling process of getting to grips with expat life thousands of miles away from home.

Regardless of their inner turmoil, you can guarantee that the Lost Souls will be bigging up 'the Dubai dream' on all of their social media accounts, even LinkedIn, with unprofessional status updates like, "Loving life! I NEVER WANT TO COME HOME," and "If I die tomorrow, scatter my ashes in the dancing fountains by the Burj Khalifa." The Lost Souls will keep up this charade while quietly crumbling inside, despite their best efforts to settle in by attending a brunch now and again, and showing up so late at Sandance that they've missed the headline act.

In reality, the Lost Souls don't know what they're doing, or why they often find themselves hanging out with fellow middle-aged, balding divorcees at the bar, who always end up initiating conversations with voluptuous women thirty years their junior. And that's because the Lost Souls are in a constant state of confusion about almost everything… with the exception of simple and, most importantly, familiar habits – whether that's microwave popcorn and E! reruns of *Keeping Up with the Kardashians,* or throwing themselves into a Dickens' novel. These they pursue with unadulterated passion, mostly for the temporary moments of distraction they bring. Indeed, it is sad that all of those sun-kissed, social, seriously fun possibilities of Dubai life pass the Lost Souls by because they're too busy hoovering the rug on their tiled floors.

Most likely to convince themselves that...

"Moving to Dubai has given me a whole new lease of life. Most people gain weight when they come here but, for the first time in 25 years, I can see my feet when I look down."

"What people don't understand about me is that I can't just sit still. I might have never lived anywhere but London before now, but I've always been restless. I've always daydreamed about palm trees, sandy shores, and a very long, exhilarating highway, just like the Sheikh Zayed Road."

"I know leaving my family and friends, selling my house, my car, and even my dog to move here was the best decision I have ever made. I am sure of that each time I get in a taxi. Every ski lesson at the Mall of the Emirates. And whenever I get my trousers tailored in Satwa for Dhs90."

Popular hangouts

The mini market, five minutes away from home, where a Lost Soul spends half-an-hour pondering whether to buy a can of Coke or Diet Coke.

Jumeirah Beach, in the foetal position, and staring out to sea to reflect on the meaning of their lives (until the Burj Al Arab proves too damn distracting).

Novo Megaplex at Ibn Battuta Mall, finding solace at a near-empty screening.

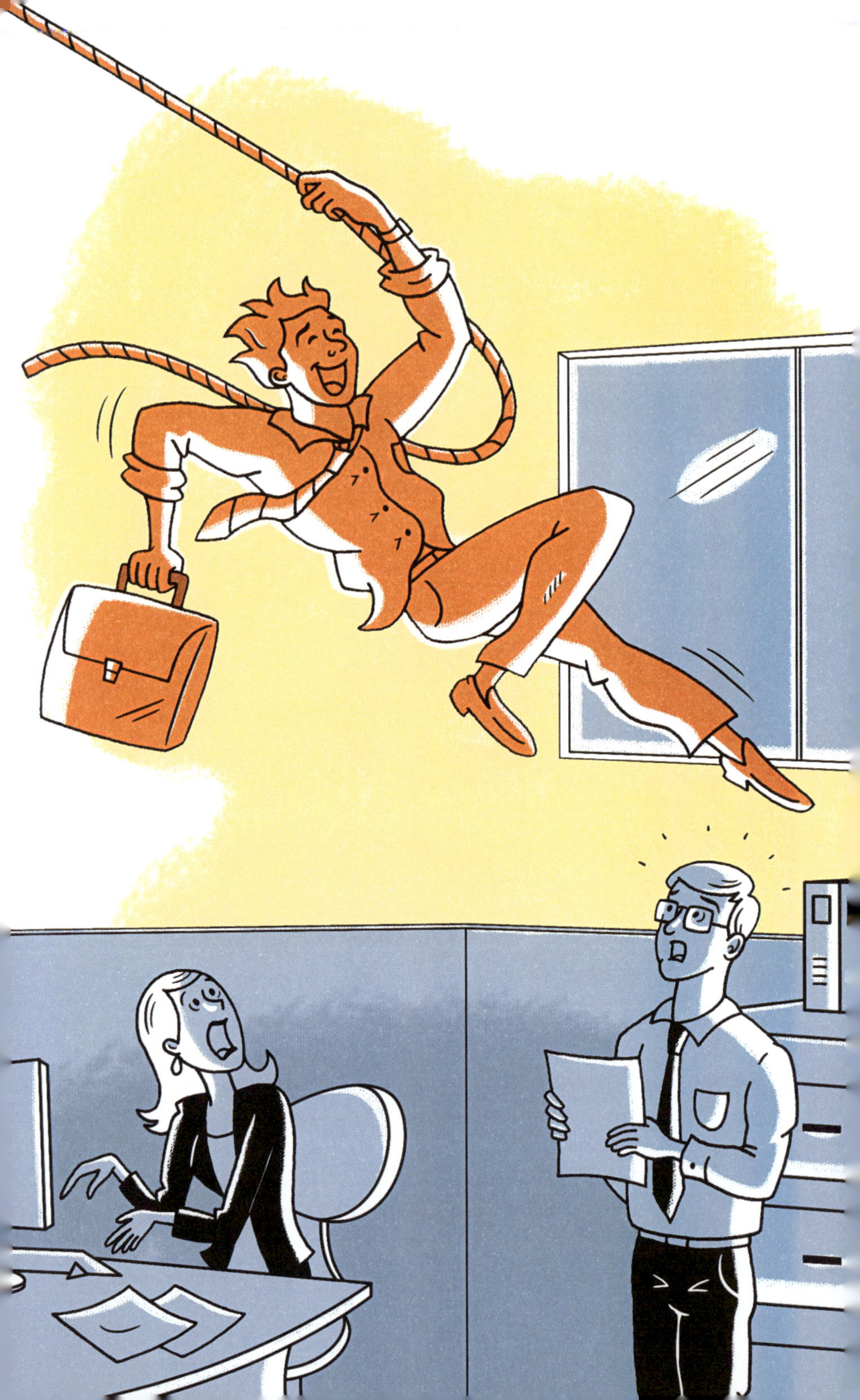

The Explorers

No other expat values Dubai's advantageous geographical position like the Explorers. Indeed, it is the city's prime locale in the Middle East, perfect for travelling to so many wonderful countries within easy reach, that drives an Explorer's decision to set up camp in the emirate. While having a great job offer, and the perks of tax-free living by the sea come as a welcome bonus, they are not as alluring as the potential opportunities to throw oneself into Emirati culture, hop across the border to Oman, or even pop over to India, Kenya or Sri Lanka for the weekend.

The Explorer struggles to focus on everyday life, and doesn't cope well with mundane routines. While taking the bin bags to the rubbish shoot or filling in work expenses, the Explorers are most certainly visualising their descent into Mauritius or checking FlyDubai's website for bargain flights every time the boss is out of sight. The Explorers have a constant wanderlust that never feels fully satisfied, not even after completing the Marathon des Sables in Morocco, the most gruelling foot race on Earth. The Explorers always need more. Almost as soon as one exotic adventure is over, they feel the intense urge to explore another corner of the globe, just as other expats might constantly crave trips to Nasimi beach, hubbly bubbly at sunset on Marina Walk, or yet another knock-off bag from Karama.

While the Explorers might have their heads, both metaphorically and literally, in the clouds, few other expats make the most out of their time in Dubai as much as these adventurous free spirits do. The Explorers might be ensconced within the city's work-hard, play-hard culture, but their Dubai bucket list doesn't include a night in with a box set and greasy takeaway. Even if they're exhausted (read: jetlagged) from their ongoing travels, they will still cram every second with sightseeing around their 60-hour working week. The Explorers share the Culture Vulture's (see page 64) passion for getting under the skin of Emirati culture, and also become experts on the traditional cuisine and the local customs. So while you'll witness all sorts of expats from all corners of the globe flocking to brunches on the weekend, you're more likely to find the Explorers chatting to local craftsmen along Dubai Creek, and supping on a refreshing camel milk smoothie in a dish-dash or an abaya.

Despite the Explorers' insatiable hunger for adventure, home will always be where the heart is. Not that they return to their native countries often, of course: they've still got 20 countries to tick off before they leave Dubai once and for all.

Most likely to say...

"I hear it's 44°C and 90 percent humidity? Can't wait to embark on this charity walk to Muscat!"

"Personally, I prefer swimming to Abu Dhabi. Beats the E11 every time!"

"It felt amazing to be skydiving over the marina's skyscrapers. Man, it's just one of the best feelings ever! I filmed the whole thing - you can watch it on my Vimeo page."

Popular hangouts

Local House Coffee Shop & Restaurant in Al Bastakiya, munching on a camel burger.

Kinokuniya at The Dubai Mall, lapping up the latest travel magazines and books for hours on end to plan the next month of adventures.

Sunset Beach (Umm Suqeim to those who aren't in the know), catching the waves at sunrise.

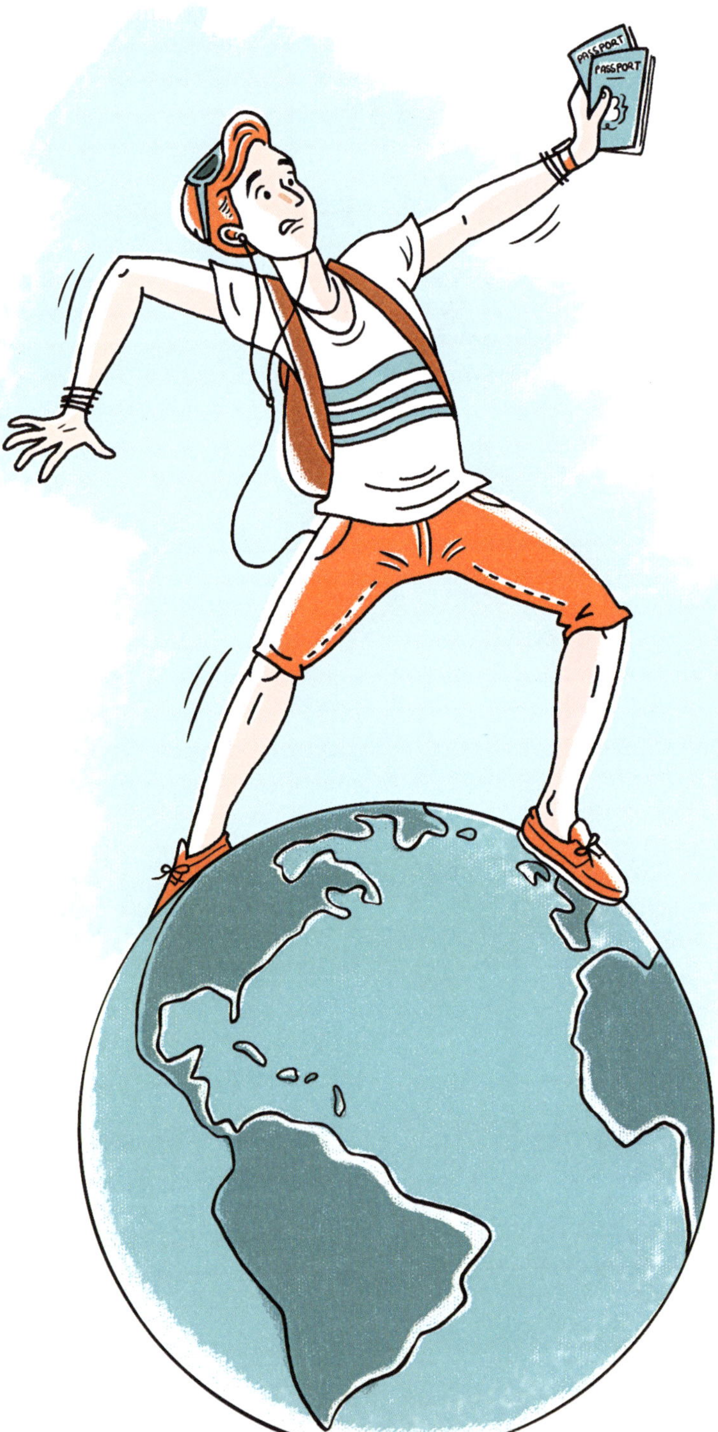
PASSPORT
PASSPORT

The Third Culture Kids

With a strong presence all over the world, the Third Culture Kids are one group of expats that are particularly popular in Dubai. The TCKs, in short, are too cool for school. So much so, they've even got their very own acronym. Every one of them has a different story, of course, but ultimately you're a Third Culture Kid if you grow up in a country and culture outside your parents' origin. Empowered with a deep understanding of all (three) cultures, the TCKs are in a constant state of confusion. Existentialist questions about where you're from, who you are, and what it all means in today's globalised world, are your badges of honour.

With around 90 percent of the population consisting of expats, it's no wonder that the TCKs are booming in Dubai. Of course, their parents' promotions and bumper job packages, not to mention (almost) 365 days of sunshine a year might have something to do with it, too. Once the emirate's TCKs complete their education and break free from the privileged confines of Dubai College, Horizons English School, Gems Dubai American Academy et al, they fall into three different categories:

1. Those who head straight for the American University of Dubai. Or the University of Sharjah if they can bear to leave their beloved emirate, or can hack the regularly congested commute.

2. Those who want to either study in the country where one, or both, of their parents are from, or who just want to study

at prestigious universities somewhere new. The TCKs in this category are keen to set up a life elsewhere.

3. Those who do the Harvard or Cambridge University thing and boomerang back to the emirate to make their own impression on the city's ambitious landscape. These TCKs often manage to launch a start-up business that's destined for great things, having already been profiled in *Forbes* before you can say, "MAKE Business Hub!" (see The Start-Up Stars on page 88).

These culturally enriched, identity-confused souls often feel hard done-by despite their prosperous suburban upbringings in Arabian Ranches, The Meadows, and Mirdif. Whether they're struggling to understand their sense of self, wish they hadn't upped sticks and moved to the Middle East in the first place, or begrudge the fact that they have family, friends, and belongings scattered around the world, the TCKs often wish life was a little more straightforward. They can wax lyrical on their jet-set lifestyle, speak fluently in almost three languages, and showcase unparalleled open-mindedness to the nth degree to impress non-TCKs living in the emirate. But, deep down, the TCKs wish they were more like you, and often wish that they could give it all up for one home, one passport, and one holiday a year. After all, juggling numerous cultures and dealing with an identity crisis of post-modern proportions can be hard work.

Most likely to say...

"Where am I from? Well, I'm... you could say... To be honest, I have no idea how to answer that. Can we just pretend that I've given you a satisfactory response and talk about what we're going to have for lunch instead?"

"I will soon have enough air miles to buy an Airbus 380. And all from just visiting family! All those hours spent in the air feel totally worth it now."

"Fancy coming around for dinner? I can offer you halloumi meshwi to start, roast beef and all the trimmings for the main, and a bar of camel milk chocolate for dessert."

Popular hangouts

Dubai International Airport, trying to find a space in one of their passports for a Dubai entry stamp.

Logged into Skype until the early hours, working with a strict 10-minute-per-person chat itinerary across three different time zones.

An exclusive meet-up for Dubai's TCKs at an art exhibition-cum-hip-hop-night at a warehouse somewhere in Alserkal Avenue.

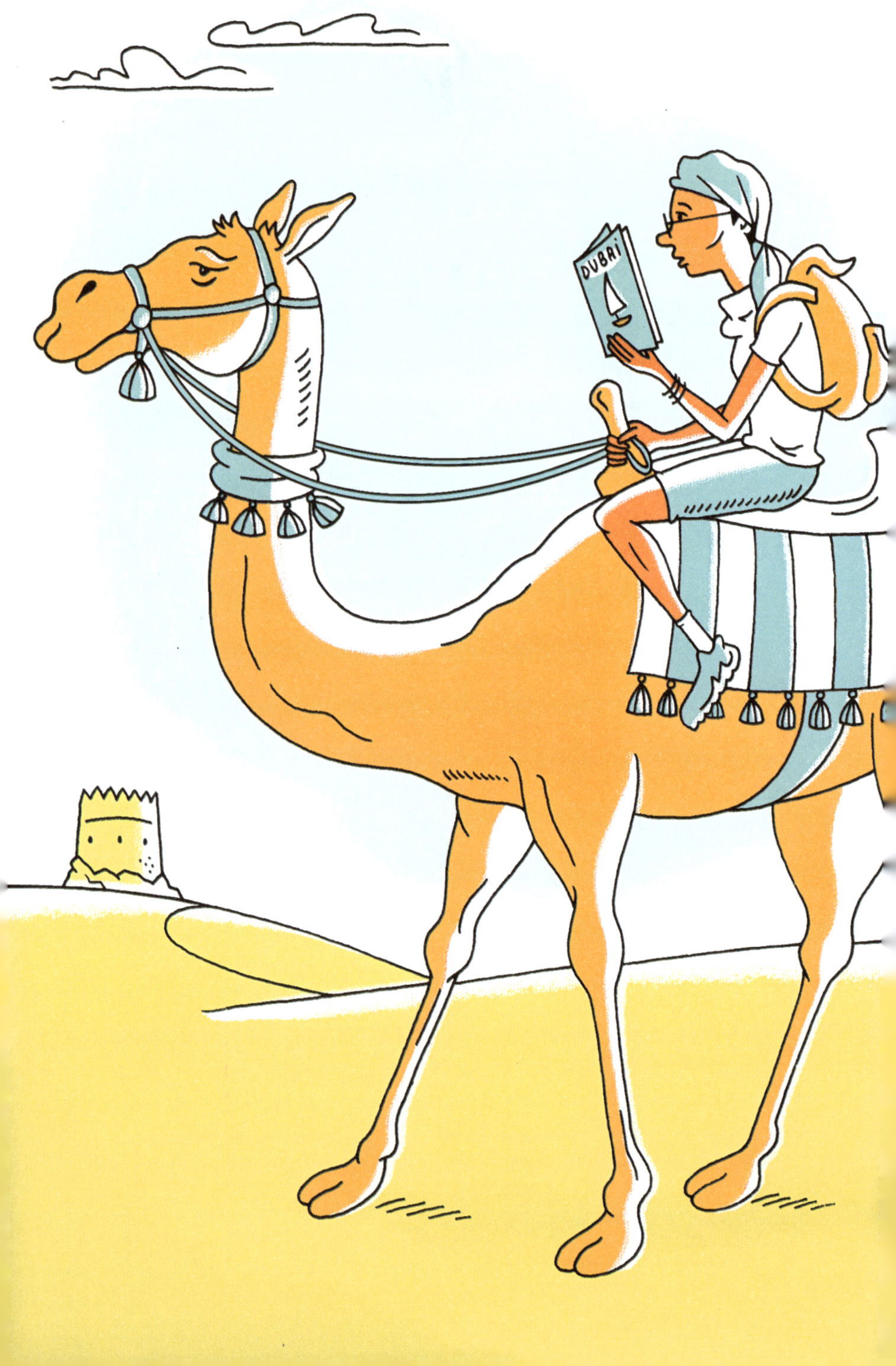
DUBAI

The Culture Vultures

You might find family and friends back home, who have never visited Dubai, asking you whether the city is a "cultural vacuum". That's probably because their knowledge of the emirate revolves around TV programmes, pictures, and articles that depict New Dubai: the shiny skyscrapers, the super-sized shopping malls, and the super-fast cars. Poor Old Dubai – the creek, the historic neighbourhood of Al Bastakiya, the white-washed pathways, and the souqs seem forgotten among the pages of a history book. A lot of people probably have no idea that the Dubai Museum exists, or that the city even has museums full stop. Cue the Culture Vultures, who never tire of discovering how the emirate came to be.

These fiercely loyal expats will defend Dubai's cultural scene to the hilt should anyone dare describe the city as a "superficial, soulless sandpit" in their presence. Their regular haunts include Art Dubai ("Oh my, what a glorious meeting of artistic minds in the desert!"), The Dubai Film Festival ("I long for this celebration of the region's best cinematic talent, both on-and-off screen!") and trips to Book Munch for the regular Dubaiophiles book club ("Such an interesting crowd. It's wonderful to hang out with actual Emiratis in a bookish setting!"). The Culture Vultures can never get enough of the city's cerebral pleasures, so much so that they fear the onset of ennui whenever they are unable to pursue them. You will never find a Culture Vulture who isn't giving his or her brain cells a fine workout, be it in the form of workshops, courses or inspiring talks. Most of them pursue several new Emirati-inspired interests at the same time. This means that it's perfectly normal for your Culture Vulture pal to be excelling at Arabic calligraphy at The Archive, dabbling in a spot of carpet design at Creekside, and flourishing in Arabic conversation classes in Knowledge Village.

The Culture Vultures love to roam Dubai Creek, to feel at one with how their beloved adoptive city evolved. But nothing can compete with the serenity the Culture Vultures feel when they swap frenetic city life for moments of solitude in the desert. Here, they relish the opportunity to observe the camels in their natural environment, the grains of sand beneath their fingertips, and the warm glow of the setting sun caressing their faces. The Culture Vultures are reluctant to divert their attention from this moment, and yet, sometimes, inspiration proves too much and they start to sketch the scene on parchment. Wearing their traditional threads in the colours of the United Arab Emirates' flag, handmade by a group of Emiratis they play backgammon with on the creek, the Culture Vultures see no better way of ending the day than smoking a hookah pipe underneath the stars.

Once back in the city, the Culture Vultures return to their villas, usually in the 'real Dubai' neighbourhoods of Satwa or Umm Suqeim, feeling rejuvenated and whole again. That's before a hankering for salty sea air and warm waves lapping at their feet brings them to the beach, carrying the life-sized dhow they made in their spare time. From here, they set afloat, travelling wherever the tide takes them.

Most likely to say...

"I don't do malls. And I cannot fathom other human beings who move here solely to while away the hours wandering in and out of shops in what are essentially ubiquitous greenhouses. They should be unearthing the authentic Arabian experience. It's not normal. And, quite frankly, it's these people who are to blame for some of the media's assumptions that this city is soulless. It makes me so angry, I've got to go and do some weaving now to calm down. I've nearly finished making my own laundry basket."

"A lot of people scoff when I say that Dubai could be the culture capital of the world in 2020. It's all about the Expo. They just don't understand the emirate's potential. It's a shame. But they're too busy sunning themselves by the Burj Al Arab, their distorted symbol of 'culture'. Pah! If only they knew. They'll see. In 2020, if not before."

"Nothing pleases me more than watching a camel, wild and free in its natural desert surroundings, as I sit on the sand in silence with a glass of milk fresh from its udders."

Popular hangouts

Making the monthly pilgrimage to Hatta Heritage Village, which dates back several thousands of years and also happens to be a particularly pleasant picnic spot.

Taking an abra repeatedly between the Dubai Creek and Deira, to discuss what 'culture' means to the people they meet so that they can write a thesis on the subject.

Alserkal Avenue, hopping from one gallery to another.

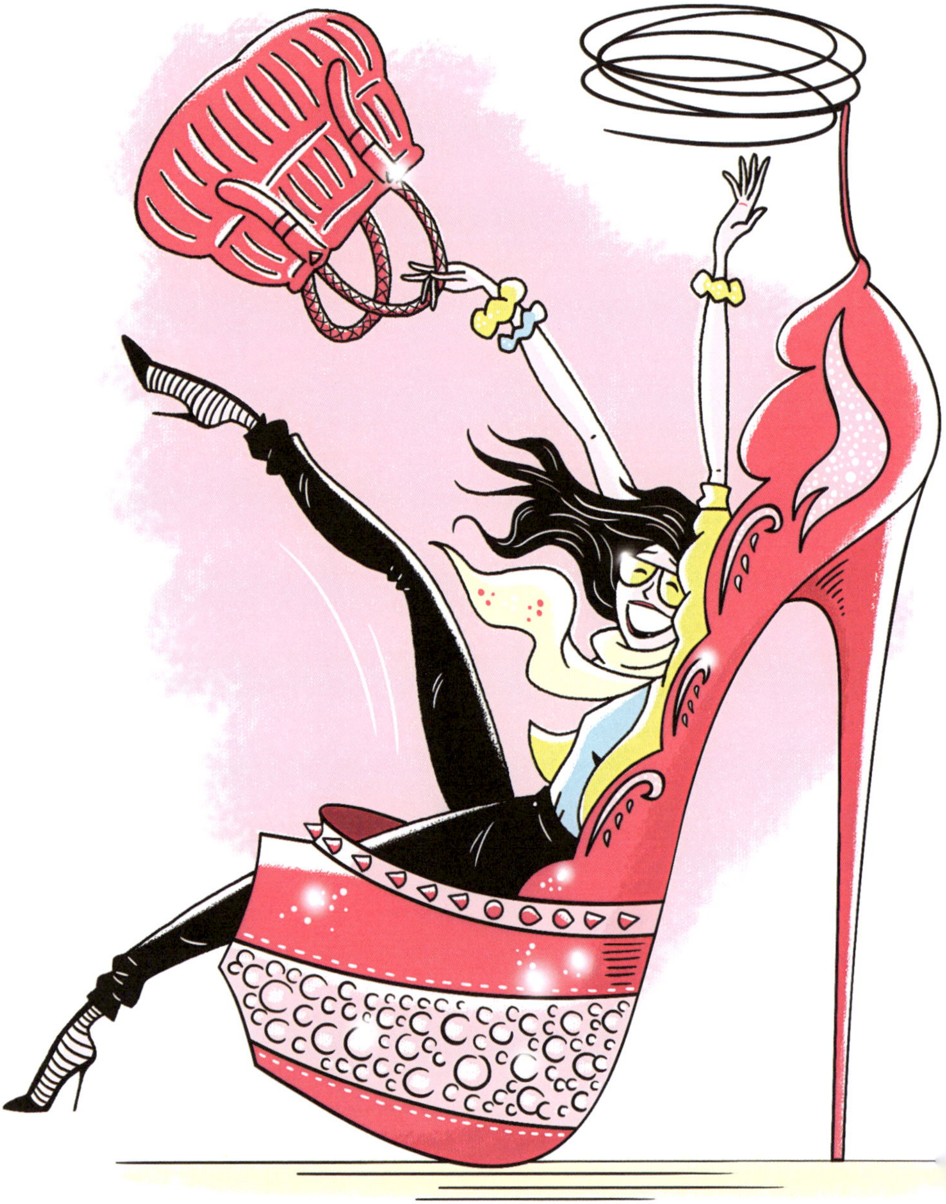

The Designer Devotees

"Ohhhhhh, it's on the website!" a Designer Devotee squeals. "Ohhhh, it's so preeeetty."

"You simply have to buy it," says a fellow Designer Devotee sat next to me. It's only natural to be surrounded by this high-end breed of expat when you work at a fashion magazine in Dubai.

"But I can't afford it. Ohhhh, but I want it. It's so pretty."

If only Diane von Fürstenberg knew at that precise moment that, thousands of miles away, one of her bags was causing elongated wails of excitement with an acute shrillness capable of rupturing my eardrums.

"I can lend you the money," says the fellow DD.

"Oh, that's so sweet. But I couldn't accept that sort of money."

"It's fine. You need that bag. It's an absolute necessity."

"Oh, thank you so much. I can't wait until it's *miiiine*!"

I'll give it to them: it was a pretty nice bag. Black, compact, tasselled – but I bet many of you reading this are thinking the same thing I was: *it's just a bag*. The Designer Devotees, whose hankering for haute couture is as vital to them as the air they breathe, do not, however, see it that way. To them, designer delights hold mystical life-altering potency.

Oh, the lengths the Designer Devotees will go to get their hands on the latest high-end threads. While we can try to put ourselves in their Louboutins in an attempt to understand their fascination with fashion, we probably won't at the crack of dawn when they traipse downtown to one of those exclusive Louby sales. Or when they pop to the mall before work because H&M has joined forces with another big name for a limited time only. We can, at least, give them our undivided attention on a Sunday morning when they confess that their weekend splurge on Net-a-Porter.com has left just Dhs50 in their bank account until payday. And we can attempt a convincing nod in agreement that five percent discount from a PR they know was "totes worth it".

The Designer Devotees, on the other hand, aren't quite so adept at feigning interest in conversations that do not interest them. If chit-chat doesn't touch upon high-profile collaborations, desecrating the latest catwalk collections, or determining a current Top 10 Designers list, it's game over. Thankfully, these sartorial souls surround themselves with fellow immaculately accessorised, coiffed, and dressed Designer Devotees who are on the same page, striking the same pose. The type of people who spend a Friday morning creating the ultimate high-end beach look from head to toe to sunbathe on their balconies. And who choose to spend the evening on a mall crawl, trawling the shops until a new outfit is complete for the office on Sunday morning. Such dedication comes easy to the Designer Devotees. They were born this way: to shop, to groom, to burst colleagues' ear drums with their fashion-charged cries, to wear heels that give them blisters… and they will be this way until their dying day. Life's a catwalk after all.

Most likely to wax lyrical about...

"Have you seen Victoria Beckham's new collection? I died and went to fashion heaven!"

"Oh, wow, have I got some exclusive news for you! Kate Moss and Cara Delevingne are joining forces to create their own label. Eek!"

"I went to an amaze pop-up sale on Jumeirah Beach Road. Vintage Burberry, Gucci, Prada. LOVE!"

Popular hangouts

Vogue Café, reading, err, Vogue.

Fashion Forward, on the front row, soaking up the catwalk action morning, noon, and night.

Fashion Avenue at The Dubai Mall, shopping up a storm.

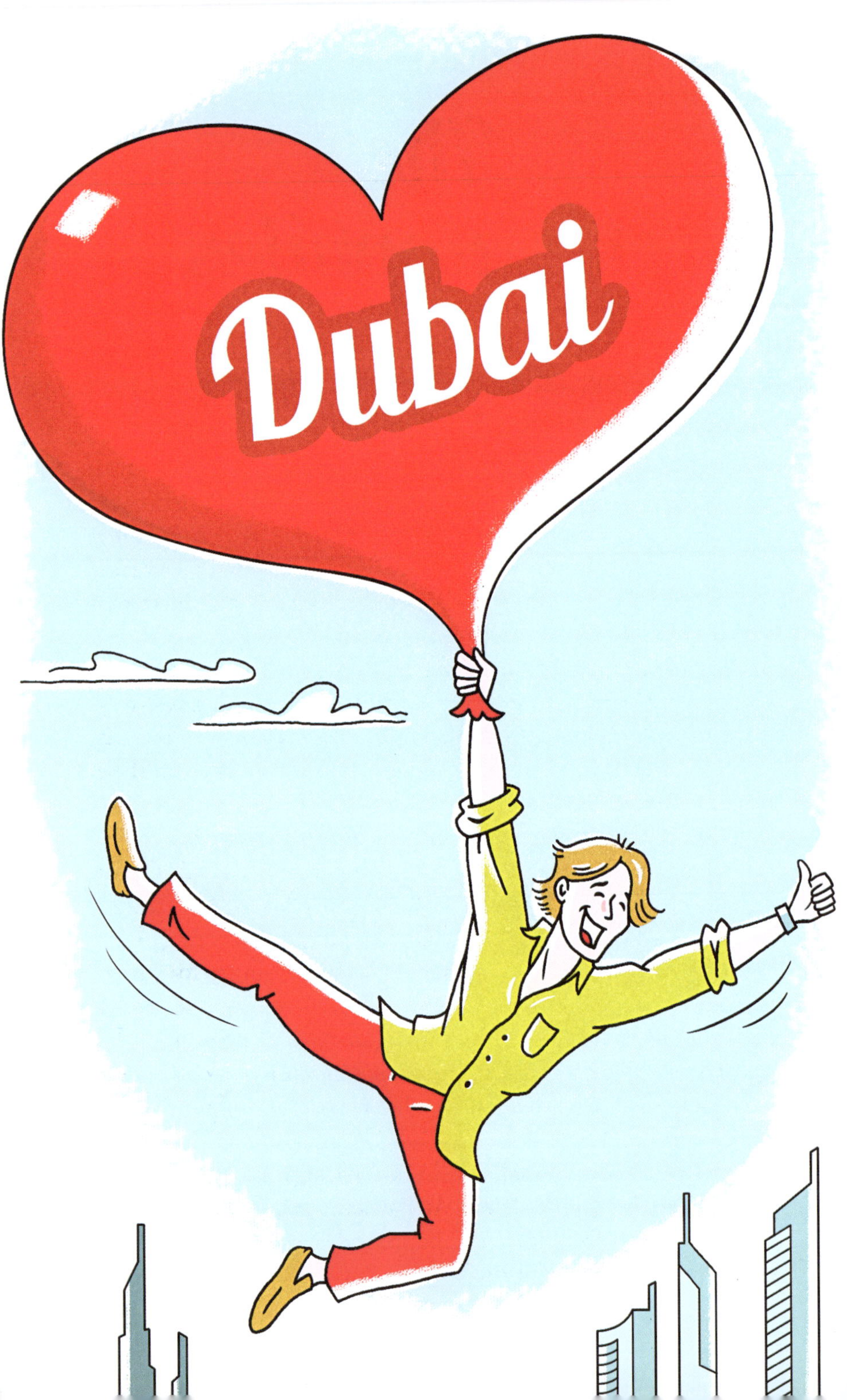
Dubai

The Dubaiophiles

For the Dubaiophile, this city can do no wrong. This expat's path to a life in the emirate is fuelled by a unique connection. Many of these expats have a burning passion for Dubai from a young age, usually nurtured by a series of family holidays. Others never visited before making the move, and yet were simply drawn to life here after reading up on Dubai or flicking through a friend's holiday snaps on Facebook. Once school or university is over, the Dubaiophiles book that one-way flight to the emirate – and dive straight into a celebratory brunch (see The Brunch Brits on page 36) the minute they arrive in their real-life vision of utopia.

Once they've indulged in brunch and unpacked their bags, the Dubaiophiles set about completing every typical Dubai experience, ticking off the latest *Time Out Dubai*'s '101 Things to Do' list as quickly as possible around their working days. Naturally every weekend is the perfect opportunity for them to focus on this personal mission. Indeed, a Saturday for a Dubaiophile could start with jumping out of a plane over Dubai Marina with Skydive Dubai. The adrenaline rush works wonders in clearing their heads from the night before. They might then go diving with sand tiger sharks at Dubai Aquarium & Underwater Zoo before a spot of lunch, shisha and backgammon with locals at Lebanese restaurant, Reem Al Bawadi, and, if they can tear themselves away from this neighbourhood favourite, they head to the desert to sand-surf at dusk. Come Sunday, the Dubaiophiles will share their weekend feats with their colleagues, describing the minutiae of every moment. Needless to say, this doesn't exactly charm, fascinate or interest long-term expats who completed their own personal Dubai bucket lists eons ago.

So eager are the Dubaiophiles that the increasing irritation of their work chums has no impact on their zealous sharing of their Dubai conquests. In fact, nothing gets the Dubaiophiles down, not even a lack of taxis after work. The Dubaiophiles feel far too lucky to be living and working in the emirate to get wound up by having to walk home in the searing heat, even when humidity has peaked at 90 percent. As far as they are concerned, any minor annoyance doesn't matter in the grand scale of things, be it a shortage of taxis, dealing with Du, or having to hoover sand off the bed sheets. All is well with the world when you can blow a month's salary on a ski-chalet suite at the Kempinski, overlooking the slopes of Ski Dubai, for you and your mates for a single night of unadulterated fun. This is a must-do event, incidentally, which most Dubaiophiles tick off within their first month in the emirate.

Should you make the fatal mistake of telling a Dubaiophile that there isn't much to do, except go to a number of beaches, malls or restaurants, prepare to be proven wrong. This is the Dubaiophile's cue to take on the role of the local tourism board. He or she see it as their duty to inform the, err, misinformed, that whatever they want to do can be done here. Whatever they want to buy, they can find it here. It's even possible to be whoever they want to be here. The Dubaiophile's energy, enthusiasm, and zest for Dubai life can be so infectious that even the most inflexible of the Reluctant Expats (see page 40) might find it hard to remain po-faced. On the other hand, the relentless Dubai spiel might push those with little patience to the edge, but hold your tongue (if possible): the Dubaiophiles are genuinely genial folk whose only crime is resolute enthusiasm for the city in which they live. It's rather endearing when you think about it. Not that the Dubaiophiles care about how you feel, of course – they're too busy enjoying themselves to even notice. If you can't beat them, join them. And if you can't join them, then ignore them!

Most likely to wax lyrical about...

"When I'm standing on my balcony at night, soaking up the view of the Palm lit up, and the yachts are rocking ever so gently in the water while massive tunes are pumping out of Barasti, I know that this is it. That there is no other place I should, or would rather, be. I was born to live in Dubai."

"After I got my nails painted in the colours of the United Arab Emirates' flag for National Day, I decided to just keep getting red, green, white, and black pedicures all year round. Dubai has already claimed my heart. Now it can have my fingernails, too."

"I'm getting the Burj Khalifa tattooed up my leg on Thursday. I. Cannot. Wait."

Popular hangouts

XL Beach Club at the Habtoor Grand Beach Resort & Spa, living it up at noon.

Dubai Marina Beach, lying in the sea, and marvelling at how hot it is all year round.

Queuing at the Immigration Department to renew their residence visas. Again.

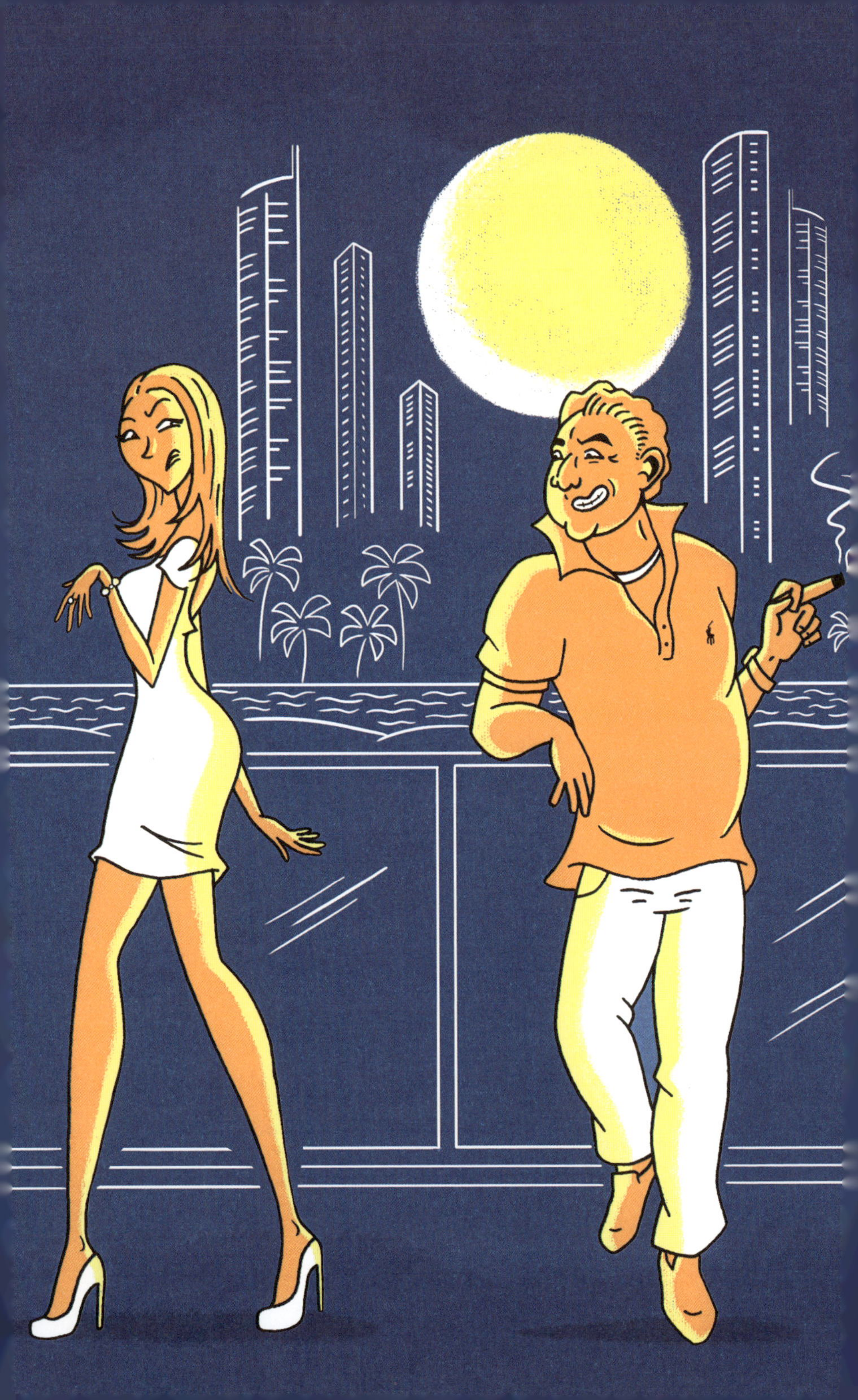

The Barasti Nasties

If you live in Dubai, Barasti, infamously known as Barnasti, needs no further introduction. But for those of you out of the loop, it's a beach bar at Le Meridien Mina Seyahi Beach Resort in Dubai Marina. Despite the 'interesting' crowd it regularly attracts after the sun goes down, it remains a popular expat hangout. Why? Because it's a convenient venue for many living and working in Media City, JBR and the Marina. The beach, where the likes of Will Smith and Jazzy Jeff reunite (OK, that was one time but it did happen), outweighs the hassle of navigating the Barasti Nasties who follow you around until you report them to the burly security guards. Long-term expats will tell you to visit Barasti in the daylight to soak up its chilled-out vibe and "very different clientele". And yet, somehow, you still end up there at night, surrounded by the overly eager Barasti Nasties who will happily provide you with the most surreal nights out of your life.

While the Barasti Nasties don't all look like clones of one another or necessarily come from the same countries, they miraculously seem to belong to a secret clique. Members have hair oozing with gel, coupled with a fatal attraction for designer polos and jeans. But what really makes them so easy to spot is how they're generally pretty jittery, upfront, and vocal in their approach.

The dance floor is where the Barasti Nasties watch you shake your thing. When their gaze, which seems mysteriously endowed with X-ray vision is ready to party, it's best to pretend they don't exist. It's also advisable to keep your eyes open for their wandering octopi hands that might unexpectedly wrap themselves around your waist. Sometimes being trapped in this suction-cup-powered grip warrants a karate chop, or equally nifty ninja move.

Barasti Nasties have different techniques up their sleeves, too. One might try a more subtle approach, endeavouring to disguise his wayward ways until the night doesn't go as planned. So keep this in mind, even when it seems like you're chatting to a seemingly sane person. You can easily tell if you've got a Barasti Nasty on undercover duty on your hands if he suddenly becomes frostier than the ski slope at the Mall of the Emirates and starts firing questions at you when you make your excuses to go home.

By the end of the night, you and your friends will agree that enough is enough, and that you will never set foot here again – until the following weekend that is, when one of your friends drags you back to Barnasti and the night unfolds like a never-ending *Groundhog Day* nightmare. Maybe, just maybe, next time you'll manage to try a different bar, or end up staying in with a NKD Pizza delivery and a chick flick instead.

Most likely to creep you out with…

"Where are you going? Here, with me, is the place to be."

"Why are you leaving? The night is young and there's a lot we can do…"

"You have a strong personality, like Beyoncé. Let me be your Jay-Z."

"You. Me. Late-night takeaway on my balcony."

"Hey girls, do you want a lift? Beautiful ladies shouldn't walk home alone."

Popular hangouts

Rock Bottom Café at the Ramee Rose Hotel in Tecom, watching you belt out a tune.

Any and every gig at Atlantis the Palm, hiding in the shadows on Nasimi Beach.

Lingering in Barnasti's car park at closing time.

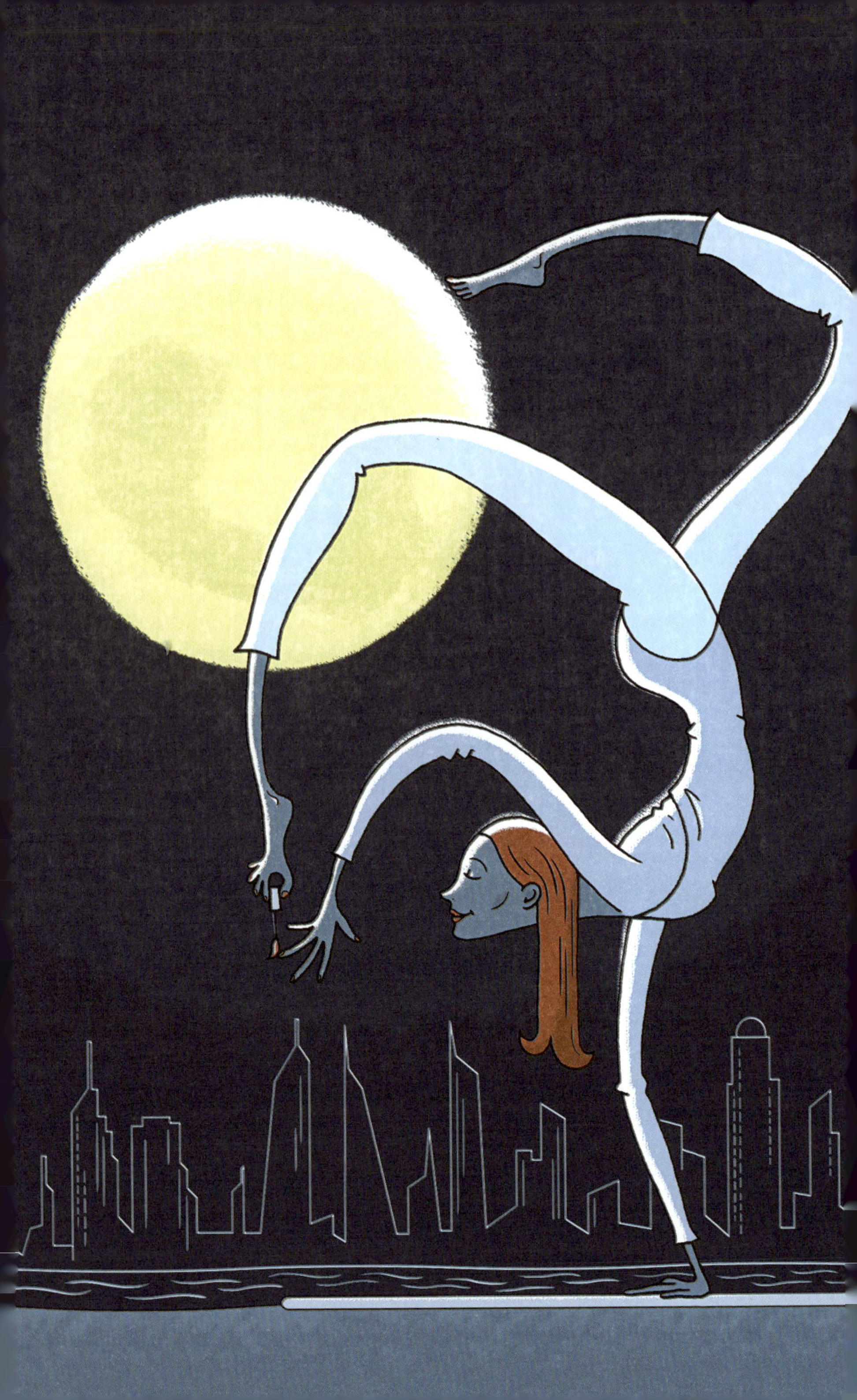

The Yogis

Maybe it's the long working hours. Or the endless potential for yoga on the beach, under the soothing glow of a full moon. Perhaps it's even the generously warm-to-far-too-hot climate that makes Bikram Yoga possible outdoors, something that is impossible in most countries. Whatever it is, the yoga scene is booming in the emirate, and subsequently, so are the Yogis.

The office is a breeding ground for these extraordinary flexible folk. I knew of a woman who regularly attended yoga with her editor at the end of a working day. The editor's wife, meanwhile, quit journalism to dedicate herself to the practice of yoga. Could there be something in the water in Dubai? Perhaps. A Yogi can convert colleagues to the brilliance of asanas (that's yoga positions) by the mere mention of how they really couldn't carry on working 14-hour days without a monthly 'Buy 10 Yoga Sessions, Get 10 Free' deal in Tecom. After all, regular trips to Tecom sounds like an easy enough solution to a bones-are-creaking, back-is-throbbing, stressed-out soul, (such as your standard Media City Mogul, page 20). Before you know it, more of your work pals are darting downtown to Urban Yoga because some bloke called Michael Gannon, who, as you might expect, also had his life transformed by yoga, is in town for a couple of days and they have heard "great things" about his teaching style. *Et voila*, your work chums become hooked, and go on to preach the wonders of yoga like a true

The Yogis

Yogi with all their chakras glowing.

Other than busy work schedules, the city's Yogis face certain obstacles that are a matter of life or death, regardless of whether they are open-minded veterans or the recently converted. They are confronted with the ever-pressing challenge of choosing which style of yoga to do, where to get their yoga on, and whether to mix it up or stay with one teacher. Each choice has the power to open the door to a different cosmic universe. As with a lot of things in life such as food (see the Foodies on page 84) and shopping, Dubai offers the Yogi too much choice. Sometimes the Yogis become confused as to whether they're more Ashtanga, Bikram, Detox Yoga Budi, or Moksha. Or whether they should give pilates a chance or BODYBALANCE™ a go (which combines pilates, yoga and even tai chi for good measure). When the number of options becomes overwhelming, the Yogis find it easier to simply unroll their mat, place it upon their tiled living room floor and do the first workout that pops up when they search 'Yoga' on YouTube. Saying that, there is one annual occasion where ample choice is more than welcomed by the Yogi community and that's Yogafest: a two-day event that a Yogi looks forward to like no other time of year. It's a chance for the Yogis far and wide to come together, to try out various types of yoga and teachers, to bond with fellow Yogis, and to be bombarded with leaflets on classes they should join and promotions that they should snap up.

Because yoga is a lifestyle, and not just a form of exercise, clean living is the Yogis' other greatest passion in life. It's Organic Foods and Café over fast-food joints any day of the week for these predominantly pescetarians, vegans, and vegetarians. The term 'Dubai stone' (see the Yo-Yo Dieters on page 28) is completely lost on the naturally slender Yogis, who are burning calories 24/7 while downing all those fresh organic vegetable juices and securing those all-important eight hours of sleep per night. Some Yogis even get their maids involved in their strict regime – you know, by mashing up the legumes, converting the tenth spare room into a totally zen zone, that sort of thing.

When the Yogis aren't in Dubai or visiting their native homes, you'll find them on a beach in Kerala, in the Pendant Pose, at their favourite yoga retreat. That is before they jack in corporate life altogether in favour of the Himalayas and their 500-hour yoga teacher training certificate. Namaste.

Most likely to say between ommmms...

"Sometimes I like to push my practice even further. I do this by seeing whether I can grab a bottle of water out of the fridge in the kitchen while keeping at least a big toe in the living room. Admittedly it's ended in a visit to A&E. Twice. But I like to stretch myself."

"I only tell someone that 'I'm bending over backwards' to see them when I actually am. I hear non-flexible people saying it all the time, and it really interferes with my Ananda (that means bliss, by the way)."

"I'm not trying to be profound, but yoga could solve the majority of the world's problems. So, be mindful of that."

Popular hangouts

Permanently refreshing the Yoga Dubai's Facebook page, the ultimate online hangout for the city's ultra-bendy community.

Talise Spa at the Madinat Jumeirah, dressed in a white leotard to be one with the moon at evening yoga sessions on the beach.

Apparel, the only Yoga clothing shop of its kind in the country, at the Jumeirah Centre. Panic-buying in bulk.

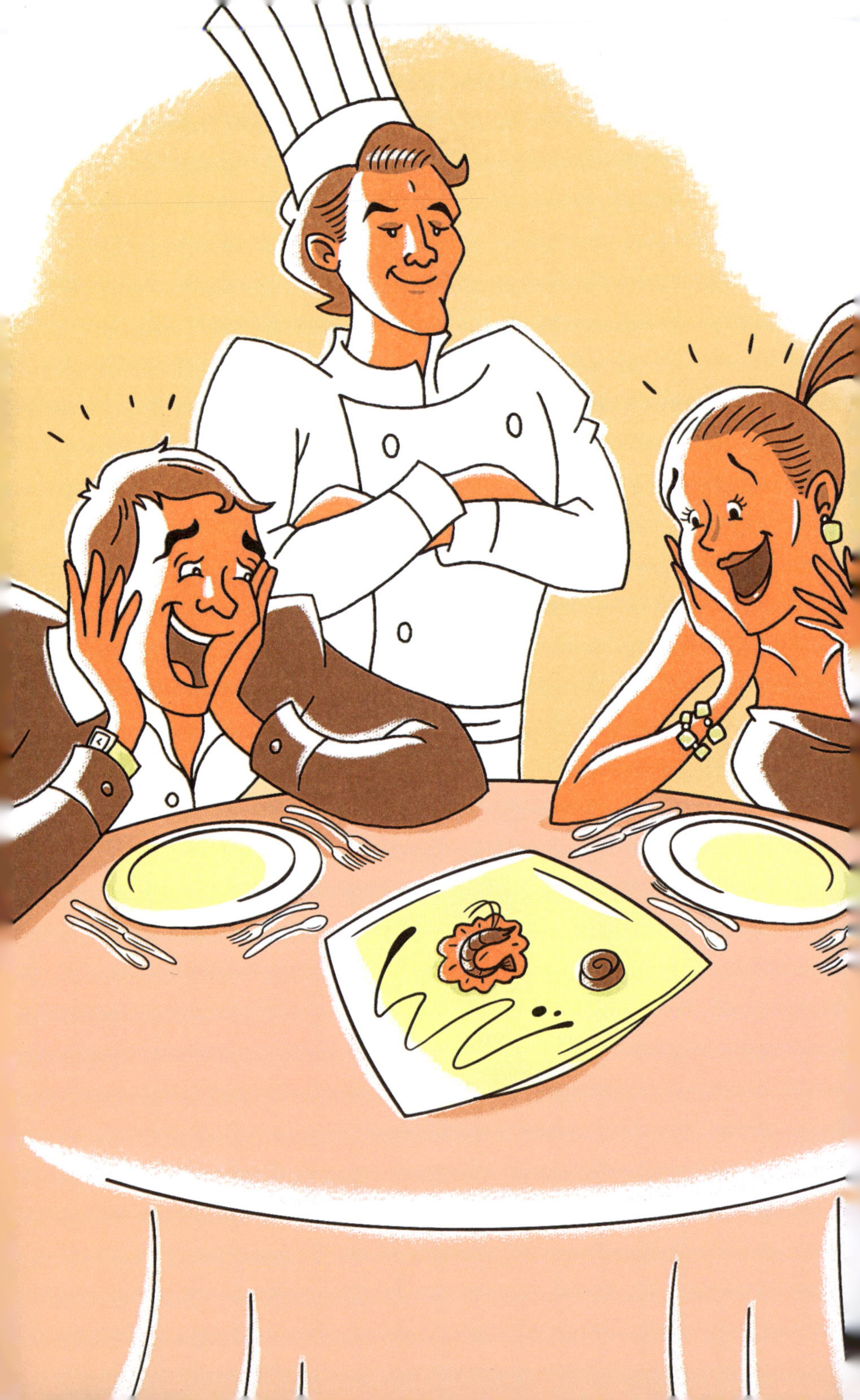

The Foodies

The Foodies are super-full on life given how much Dubai spoils them on a daily basis. Indeed, few other cities around the world can offer the Foodies what this emirate can. What other city can pride itself on such a comprehensive home-delivery culture? You can pretty much get any international cuisine of your choice delivered straight to your door or desk. And all at the click of a button, or a quick telephone call, at any time of the day.

It's also rarer than beluga caviar to have so many world-class dining venues frequently popping up with prolific chefs behind the instantly recognizable restaurant names. Even the concentration of restaurants is the embodiment of delectable temptation. The choice and pace at which new restaurants open make it challenging for even the most die-hard Foodies to keep up. This leaves them hungry for being the first to know the latest food-related news, and the first through the doors of the hippest new joint in town.

While the Foodies don't share the Yogis' (see page 80) passion for contorting their limbs, they do share an affinity with one another when it comes to their enthusiasm for organic produce. It's not unusual for Foodie and Yogi friends to bump into one another at The Farmers' Market on the Terrace at Jumeirah Emirates Towers every Friday. It's the Foodies' favourite way to kick off the weekend, stocking up on fresh seasonal vegetables so that they cook up a storm, resulting in an endless amount of leftovers, which they will show off at work. Nonchalantly, of course.

And once more, just like the Yogis, the Foodies look forward to their own short-lived fiesta: Taste of Dubai, where dirhams are swapped for vouchers. These golden tickets take enamoured Foodies to a gastronomical heaven akin to a real-world reenactment of *Charlie and the Chocolate Factory*. When the festival comes to an end, they leave knowing that they might have put on an entire Dubai stone (see the Yo-Yo Dieters on page 28) in a weekend, but at least they didn't let any food vouchers go to waste. Oh, and – having networked with culinary professionals the whole time – the Foodies ensure they bag a spot at an exclusive new restaurant opening, too. A tasty job well done, and a feast that will no doubt warrant the Foodies' secret weapon: a reliable pair of elasticated trousers.

Most likely to enthuse, in between bites...

"What sort of life is it if you can't dine at a five-star restaurant every day of the week?"

"I know La Petite Maison like the back of my hand. I could walk to my table, seat myself and order my usual scrambled duck eggs with my eyes closed and my back against my chair, which is always suitably toasty from my last visit."

"Last night, I recreated Atmosphere's afternoon tea experience at home. It was wonderful, even without the stunning views. So good that I might call up the restaurant and see if they'd like to employ me immediately. No salary necessary, but unlimited meals vital."

Popular hangouts

Rhodes Mezzanine at the Grosvenor House, to dine with Gazza, aka celebrity British chef BFF, Gary Rhodes.

Zuma, for the sumptuous sushi, the amazing ambience, and the opportunity to admire the dazzling diners that flock to this raw-fish mecca.

Waitrose, doing the weekly shop. Naturally only the most selective supermarket will do.

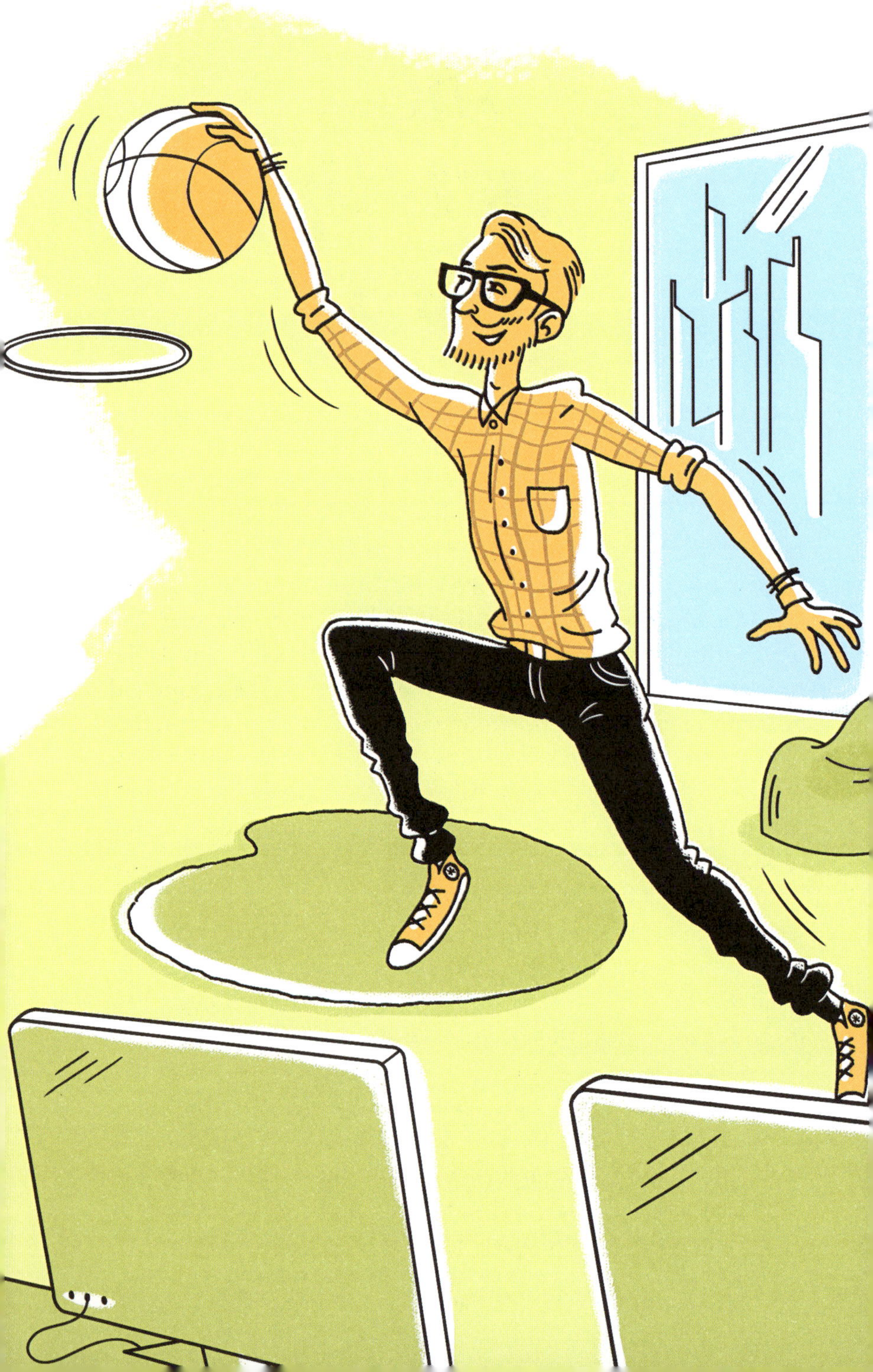

The Start-Up Stars

The Start-Up Stars thrive on being big fish in a teeny, tiny pond. They are smart, ambitious, hard-working opportunists who work morning, noon and night to create their very own empire in what he or she considers the most exciting business landscape in the Middle East.

SUSs are just as cool as the TCKs (see page 60), if not cooler, considering that their unofficial acronym indicates just how sorted they are. Plus, many SUSs are actually also TCKs returning home in a bid to take over the world. These guys and girls are convinced that throwing their dot.com into the Internet City ring is what Mark Zuckerberg would've done had he not set up camp in California's Silicon Valley. Moving shop from the maid's room to an office in Media City is the most exciting move in the world for them: it's the first step to realising long-lived dreams of international 'meeja' king and queen status. And, while some might call them "ridiculously naïve", these optimistic go-getters believe that their independent magazines will boldly buck the trend of declining print sales and be hailed as "the best print title to hit newsstands since *The New York Times*" in the, err, *New York Times*.

In Al Quoz, meanwhile, a particular species of twenty- and thirty-something entrepreneurs gravitate towards the low-key, remote, and hip vibe of the area's industrial warehouses: TCKs, who have migrated back to The Sandpit fresh from the streets of Shoreditch, London, and Bushwick, Brooklyn. These smart species are armed with impressive MBAs from London Business School and Columbia. With their thick-rimmed glasses, trendy haircuts, drainpipe jeans, and bicycles (even though consistent pavements are rarer than rain in Dubai), the TCKs-cum-SUSs hook up with fellow hybrid expat entrepreneurs to form an unrivalled creative network of masterminds. These elite entrepreneurs are guaranteed to come up with the next big eco-friendly, unique, downright ingenious company that will offer easy solutions to everyday problems and transform the globe's perception of Dubai forever more. Well, that's the plan, anyway. And they will achieve this while living up to the 10 ultimate laws of marketing, creating their own niche and establishing solid brand equity. Well, they'll give it their all, all right.

But the Start-Up Stars don't just want to make an impact on the international business arena. These image-conscious biz whizzes also require an inspired office space. If it works for Google, then it sure is good enough for these dynamic gems too. A ping-pong table is mandatory, of course, as is – at the very least – a pin-ball machine, basket ball court-cum-meeting-room, pick 'n' mix sweets zone, and a 200-seater cinema. This all works well for the Start-Up Stars considering how much time they spend in the office. Only the Media City Moguls (see page 20) have similarly indistinguishable boundaries between work, play and home (minus the nifty fold-out beds, which the Start-Up Stars have naturally fitted into the walls of their offices).

Indeed the Start-Up Stars have a hard time knowing how to handle downtime away from their wacky warehouses, endless social media streams and brainstorming sessions. That's just the way they're built. And that's OK, because before you can say "Burj Khalifa", they will have retired a few months short of the big 4-0, having built the successive tallest building in the world. By then, they will have also built up their own highly successful multi-million dirham company, and will find themselves spending the rest of their days swimming in Dhs1,000 notes in the Olympic-sized swimming pool in their back garden, which, incidentally, is as big as 10 football pitches.

Most likely to spout dubious wisdom like...

"If life gives you lemons... well, don't waste them. Slice them up, pop them in a jug of water and serve with ice. It's the small details that matter. Your clients will notice the difference and thank you later."

"'Screw it, let's do it.' That's always been my motto and I apply it to everything I do - and you should, too. It's the only way you'll ever get anywhere in this world. Technically, Richard Branson said, 'Screw it, let's do it' first but he's not here now to think about your customers' needs. I am. And anyway, I'm sure I know far more about the Middle East market than he does."

"When you're starting out in business, spend big. Don't cut back. I see these entrepreneur books that tell people that you can start your business with just Dhs500. These people are lying to you. It's worth risking nearly all the money you have in the world to reach your dreams. And if it all goes wrong? I'm sure the Loyal Bank of Mummy and Daddy will be there for you, just as it was for me."

Popular hangouts

MAKE Business Hub, considered the other home-from-home for the majority of Start-Up Stars, where they bathe in the glory of their visionary powers.

Wandering around Dubai Miracle Garden, the world's biggest natural flower garden, to mull over the Next Big Idea in peace and quiet, while surrounded by the sweet aromas of more than 45 million blooms.

JW Marriot Marquis, the tallest hotel in the world, for a power lunch in an attempt to impress potential new clients.